Effective Communication of Employee Benefits

Richard M. Coffin
Michael S. Shaw

American Management Association, Inc.

To
Jean and Bobbi

© American Management Association, Inc., 1971. All rights reserved. Printed in the United States of America.

This publication may not be reproduced, stored in a retrieval system, or transmitted in whole or in part, in any form or by any means, electronic, mechanical, photocopying, recording, or otherwise, without the prior written permission of the Association.

This book has been distributed without charge to AMA members enrolled in the Insurance and Personnel Divisions.

International standard book number: 0-8144-2149-0
Library of Congress catalog card number: 74-158465

Contents

1	This Business of Communicating	1
2	Establishing Objectives	12
3	Planning the Program	23
4	The Tools of the Trade	34
5	Measuring the Results	63
6	Communicating Overseas	78
7	Communicating About Direct Compensation	92
8	Six Case Studies	103
Appendix	Summary of Benefits Communications Practices in 202 Large Companies	119

Acknowledgments

IN RESEARCHING and writing this book, we have unblushingly drawn on the knowledge, experience, and skills of our friends and associates at Towers, Perrin, Forster & Crosby. Without attempting to categorize the contributions made by each, we would like to take this opportunity to express our extreme gratitude to John F. Abel, Joseph A. Banik, Vicki Bigish, Kyran P. Carey, John J. Davis, Cynthia L. Flansburg, Roy G. Foltz, Joyce A. Gildea, Joanne T. Hayman, Kenneth E. Heberling, Sheila M. Katze, Ronald H. Lamey, Susan R. Linder, Janet M. Linus, John C. Maydew, Toni K. O'Connell, Bruce A. Searle, and Richard L. Yake. In addition, we would particularly like to thank Thomas Gannon of the American Management Association staff for his patience and gentle encouragement throughout the course of this endeavor.

RICHARD M. COFFIN
MICHAEL S. SHAW

1

This Business of Communicating

THE boys on the construction site were taking a break one morning when the foreman shouted, "For crying out loud, Hezekiah, don't lean against that beam. You'll knock the whole works over." And just before the bricks started to tumble, Hezekiah was heard to reply, "Ce–a spus?"[1] From that point on, the Babel project went rapidly downhill to take its place in history as the first recorded victim of a communications breakdown.

In the ensuing millennia, faulty communications have led to countless other failures. Although few have been as dramatic or quite as widely publicized as the Tower of Babel, many have been equally painful for those concerned. As a result, today it is difficult to find anyone who underestimates the importance of good communications.

[1] "What did he say?"

Just about everybody agrees that we all would be better off if we communicated more effectively. And everybody is right. We would.

But if this is true, why don't we make a better job of it? Why do we still have political, social, personal, and business failures that might have been avoided if only we understood each other a little better?

The reason is that good communication is an elusive and extremely difficult goal to achieve. It hardly ever happens spontaneously—quite the contrary. Moreover, if and when you achieve it, you may be unaware that you have done so, since the usual evidence is simply a lack of the kinds of problems that poor communication engenders. Finally, even if you do achieve it and know that you have, you may still find that it doesn't last very long because so many things can impair or destroy it.

What Is Communication?

A telephone operator, a vacuum-cleaner salesman, a skywriter, and a fortuneteller could each say quite honestly, "I'm in the communications business." So before going any further, we ought to define just what we are talking about.

Definitions of the word *communications* are legion, and range in length from several words to several pages. One of the shortest, and one which is entirely adequate for the purposes of this book, is this: *Communications is an exchange of understanding*.

This is a good definition for two reasons. First, it implies that one person alone cannot communicate. It takes at least two in order to exchange anything—one to transmit, the other to receive. And this underscores the basic fact that communication is as much a listening process as a speaking process.

Second, the definition indicates that the exchange does not involve words or pictures. It involves understanding. Consequently, the transmitter can shout his head off, but if the receiver hears only the sounds and not the meaning, there is no communication. Obvious? Perhaps, but it's remarkable how often a person who speaks thinks he is automatically communicating.

The Communication Process

Conscious communication originates in the transmitter's cerebral cortex, that part of the brain which is concerned with such complex functions as thought and memory. In the form of electrical energy, the message to be communicated then goes to other parts of the brain for processing into action, then passes down through the nervous system to emerge as sounds, gestures, or other body movements. At that point, the message makes an impact on the receiver's sensory organs, is again transformed into electrical energy, and starts back through his nervous system to his cerebral cortex. A nice, quick, reliable system. Except that somewhere along the way, the message also passes through a series of at least four filters—two belonging to the transmitter and two to the receiver. These filters add to the message, subtract from it, and distort it in various ways. And as more people become involved in the communication process, such as writers, editors, meeting leaders, or artists, the more filters the message must pass.

Unless you have a basic understanding of how these filters operate, it is extremely unlikely that the message in your cerebral cortex will reach that of the receiver without being distorted.

The language filter. Upon reading or hearing words, people frequently translate them into mental pictures.

And unless you are specific in your choice of words, you run the sometimes serious risk of the wrong picture being formed. For example, what picture do the following four words make in your mind?

Table   Cloth   Knife   Man

Quite possibly you have pictured a man seated at a table eating his dinner. But it's also possible that you have visualized a surgeon preparing to operate. If the more specific words "operating table," "gown," "scalpel," and "surgeon" had been used instead, there would be no guesswork. You would have pictured a surgeon preparing to operate, and just that.

The potential scope of the problem becomes apparent when you realize that the dictionary lists some 14,000 possible meanings for the 500 most commonly used words in the English language—an average of 28 meanings per word. Perhaps it was a similar realization that led Lewis Carroll to make Humpty Dumpty say: "When *I* use a word, it means just what I choose it to mean—neither more nor less." Would that it were only so.

But words aren't the only problem. When they are strung together in a fashion designed more to impress than express, real confusion can result. For example, what was the writer of these words trying to say?

> The resistance and reactance that are inherent in the designated engine are of such a distinct and oppositional magnitude as to prevent a flow of current sufficient to bring it up to the desired celerity, in spite of the factuality that the engine is equipped with amortisseur winding.

If you puzzle it through, the meaning becomes clear: The

motor isn't big enough for the job. And that's one point the writer was trying to make—but only one.

Even symbols can be misinterpreted. In American military circles, the symbol A-O.K. means that everything is fine. But in England it means the absence of anything, or nothing, and in parts of Latin America, it means something else entirely, which is better left unexplained here.

The experience filter. This is really a two-stage affair. At the first stage, incoming and outgoing messages are filtered according to the receiver's or transmitter's past experiences, including his social and cultural background, economic history, religious upbringing, and education, to name only a few. Together, these experiences form his own unique pattern of values, prejudices, attitudes, opinions, and gut feelings. They tell him what is right and wrong, good and evil, beautiful and ugly.

The second stage of this filter evaluates communications in terms of *present* experiences, or those things which are happening simultaneously with the communication process. It tells the receiver, for example, that when you say "Yes" you really mean "Don't bother me now" because of your distracted look, impatient tone, and the way you drum your fingers on the desk. Likewise, an announcement that states "No bonus will be paid this year due to sagging profits" will be received in one way if you concurrently announce that dividends to shareholders have been cut. Needless to say, it will be received in a much different way if you announce a dividend increase at the same time.

Trust is the most important element in keeping your communications from being distorted as they pass through the receiver's experience filter. Unless the receiver trusts you, it is very unlikely that he will believe you.

Some years ago, a large company in the South established a deferred profit-sharing plan. This was truly a first, since until that time employees had had virtually no benefits. But a new generation of management had taken over and things were improving. The profit-sharing plan was one example. Because the new management was also conscious of the value of communications, it conducted a series of group meetings to acquaint employees with the virtues of the new plan. After one such session, an elderly member of the audience approached the rather youthful meeting leader and said, "All right, Sonny. I heard all the nice things you said about this plan. Now, tell me, where's the hooker?" The meeting leader responded that there were no hookers, that the plan had been established in good faith and was even under the jurisdiction of the U.S. Internal Revenue Service. The elderly employee stared at him for a moment and replied, "Maybe you can fool some of these people, Sonny, but I've been around here long enough to know that this company doesn't give *anything* away." Then he turned and walked off.

If that man's employers expected any loyalty or appreciation from him in return for profit sharing, they were sadly mistaken. The practical message in this story is clear: To be believed, you must first be trusted. Ralph Waldo Emerson stated it aptly: "What you are sounds so loudly in my ears that I cannot hear what you say."

In coping with the experience filter, it's also important to keep in mind that what you say often isn't half as important as how you say it. Roy G. Foltz illustrates this point well in his work, *Management by Communication* (unpublished).

> In the case of three people habitually late for work, you don't have to tell them all to "get the hell to work on time." You are probably well advised to be selective in what you say to each of them.

To the guy who wanted your job: "I get to work on time. Why can't you?"

To the long-service employee: "We need you to be an example for the younger people."

To the guy who's often depressed: "Up and at 'em, tiger."

Gearing your message to the individual may take a little more effort, but it usually produces much better results.

Challenges to Good Communications

Even when you make the most diligent efforts to minimize the effects of the filtration, your message may still go awry, since there are other obstacles to contend with. Almost any good communications manual will list at least several dozen of them, but rather than repeat what is readily available from other sources, we will discuss only those obstacles that pose particular challenges to the communicator of information about benefits.

One such challenge stems from the fact that the manner in which employee benefits are designed can have a marked influence on their communications potential. To take a simple illustration, consider two companies with the identical objective of providing hospital room and board benefits equal to the current semiprivate rate. One of them expresses the benefit in terms of a dollar-per-day amount, while the other states that its plan pays the full cost of semiprivate hospital accommodations. When hospital room rates increase, the first company can raise benefits by a like amount, and then tell employees that their coverage has been increased. But for the second company there has been no apparent change—even though an equal increase was granted.

A somewhat comparable situation exists with retirement plans which determine benefits by means of a final average earnings formula as opposed to a dollar-per-month formula or a career average earnings formula with periodic updating of past service benefits.

Other design factors can also influence communications. Waiting periods for eligibility in various plans may be purposely spread out over a period of months or years in order to create more legitimate opportunities to communicate about them. There are also some people who believe that employees are both more aware and more appreciative of plans to which they contribute than they are of plans which are financed entirely by their employers.

Of course, none of this means that communications about benefits should dictate the design of those benefits. There are many good reasons for full semiprivate hospital provisions, final average earnings formulas, uniform eligibility requirements, and noncontributory benefits. But in weighing those reasons, you should consider their implications for effective communications.

Another challenge arises from the subject matter itself. For the most part, benefits are simply not very pleasant topics for communication. Holidays and vacations evoke happy images in most employees' minds, but the benefits communicator usually deals with more disturbing subjects, such as death, retirement, or disability.

Approaches to this problem vary. Some communicators prefer to treat benefits work with a light touch, hoping it will offset part of the unpleasantness of the subject matter. But the smiling widow who appears in so many group life insurance booklets leaves other communicators cold. They take a more sober stance, feeling that a serious subject requires a serious treatment. What is best in a given situation ought to be based on the expected reaction of the people for whom the communication is intended. Frequently, that will be determined by their age. Generally speaking, the closer people come to the realities of retirement or death, the less likely they are to take them lightly.

Benefits also challenge the communicator because they are usually founded on contracts and other legal documents. Since such instruments are usually designed to cover all possible contingencies and to subtract from their substance all possible meanings save one, they tend to be written in long, complex legalese. Translating them into language that is equally acceptable to house counsel and an 18-year-old file clerk is no small task. It requires discriminating judgment, a fair degree of writing skill, and a thorough grounding in the techniques of benefits communications.

The functional method of describing benefits is one such technique. It was developed to cope with the fact that many benefit plans provide more than one kind of coverage. Benefits for total and permanent disability, for example, might be available from a disability plan, a profit-sharing plan, a retirement plan, and a life insurance plan, as well as from Social Security.

But the traditional method of describing benefits is to group all provisions of a plan in one place, such as a booklet or section thereof. Thus, an employee might have to search through a number of different references to find information about his total benefits. Using the functional method, however, the grouping is done according to the various functions the benefits perform; in other words, it is arranged by events that might beset the employee, like total and permanent disability. Thus, a booklet entitled *What You Get if You Become Disabled* would explain the pertinent provisions of several different plans.

Although a functional description of benefits is not well suited to all benefit programs—for example, those with optional participation in some plans or those without reasonably uniform eligibility requirements—an increasing number of companies seems to be using that approach.

Of course, the first goal of any communication is to capture the attention of the person for whom it is intended. And this is becoming more and more difficult. The problem is noise. It has been estimated that in the course of a single day the average adult American spends 45 minutes reading his newspaper, that his television set plays for six hours, and that his radio is on for two and one-half hours. During his waking moments, he is exposed to some 1,500 commercial messages, nearly 100 an hour.

Breaking through this sound barrier is no easy trick. The company publication sent to the employee's home must compete for his attention with *Time* magazine, *Popular Mechanics,* or *Playboy,* any or all of which may arrive in the same mail. Similarly, he is likely to judge the booklet you publish about benefits by the same standards he applies to a slick, well-illustrated mutual fund brochure produced by a top advertising agency. Therefore, what you communicate to him must be visually inviting, well-prepared, and pertinent to his informational needs. If it's dull, drab, and printed in undersized type, you can be sure he won't read it for lack of something else to occupy his attention.

Benefits communications will also be affected by the way the entire corporate communications function is organized ("disorganized" might be a more appropriate word in some cases). Obviously, the responsibility to communicate must be shared by many. But unless guidelines are set forth in the form of policy statements and coordination of the total effort is carefully supervised, communications can become a hodgepodge of many corporate voices proclaiming points of view that may not always coincide. Consider, for instance, the company which announced a savings bond drive (through the treasurer's office), a charity campaign (through the personnel department), and a new employee-pay-all long-term disability plan (through the benefits department), all to start in the same pay period.

Where should the overall responsibility for communications be vested? The answer will depend on the nature and structure of each organization, but the ideal place is at the very top of the corporate ladder. Lynn A. Townsend, chairman of Chrysler Corporation, apparently agrees: "It is the chief executive who must establish the right communications climate. It is he who must make clear that such an investment is not an on-again, off-again proposition."

Perhaps the greatest challenge of all to good communications lies in the fact that employee benefits, like so many other aspects of people management, are constantly being acted upon by new knowledge, desires, and values. In recent years, for example, we have learned from the behavioral scientists that benefits and other forms of compensation no longer motivate employees, that in fact they never did. Government representatives tell us that private pensions and insurance will soon be obsolete. And we hear from campus recruiters that, according to college students, benefits just aren't "where it's at."

Challenges such as these will strain the resources of the benefits communicator as never before. He will have to be better educated in his business and better equipped to carry it out. He may even have to help develop better products to communicate about. In short, he will have to work harder than ever to achieve that elusive and difficult goal of good communications.

2

Establishing Objectives

WHY is the communication function in industry usually not accorded the status of production or sales? One reason may be that senior management is unable to evaluate it. What is communication worth? What does it achieve in financial terms? In measuring the value of communication, it's difficult to apply the yardsticks used to measure performance and productivity in other activities. However, the notion of developing firm objectives for communicating information about benefits has gained increasing acceptance since the adoption by many organizations of the concept of management by objectives.

Establishing communication objectives is not difficult. It basically boils down to the simple question: Why are we communicating? Or, to be more precise: What do we want our communication to accomplish?

Developing a Formula

Just as no cut-and-dried system exists for communicating with all employees, so no one standard formula can be used for increasing sales or productivity. But a key characteristic of any sales or production drive is a firm statement of exactly what is to be attained. Whether the goal is expressed in terms of rupees or widgets, and the time span in minutes or months, objectives are set—and they are set in concrete terms. They may be divided into short-term, medium-term, and long-term goals. At different points in the program, and certainly at the end of the program, they serve as the basis for an evaluation of results.

Communication objectives, on the other hand, are rarely set in such concrete terms. Often they are not established at all, although in many situations the objectives are obvious. For example, the memo to an employee asking him to handle a charity fund drive is clearly written with the intention of achieving his acceptance. Too often, however, no effort is made to establish objectives for communicating information about benefits. Projects and programs are launched without a clear understanding of what they are intended to achieve.

Frequently the effort is made simply to meet legal requirements for communicating to employees the basic terms and provisions of a pension or profit-sharing plan. Other times it is designed to acquaint employees with changes in benefits. But to what extent? And to what real purpose?

Many companies embark on comprehensive programs to increase employee awareness of their benefits immediately prior to labor negotiations, or simply because management has a vague impression that employees are unable to place a monetary value on their benefits. These reasons are probably worthy enough, but they lack a concrete purpose or quantitative definition. Thus, even when an imaginatively conceived and well-executed program is launched, its effectiveness cannot be measured in any but subjective terms.

Ages of Employees

Perhaps the company develops the program to reach its younger employees, who tend to see their compensation only in direct, tangible terms. When this basis is used, much of the program's effect is wasted, because the majority of employees are older people with longer service records. Thus, an expensive broad-brush approach may be much less effective than a more limited effort directed at new employees. In some situations a more judicious use of media may achieve better results. In other words, whenever a program goes off the rails, the chances are that its objectives were not carefully established before implementation.

Basically, those objectives are determined by the answers to these questions: Who should receive information about benefits? How much? When? How often?

The answers obviously depend on a number of factors which will rarely be the same for any two organizations. Various levels of management, or of age and income groups, or of employees and nonunion groups—all these groups will have different information needs.

In most organizations, a major factor is the extent to which supervisors are considered a source of information about benefits. In companies where management authority is delegated widely, a concerted effort is required to train and maintain front-line supervisors as knowledgeable and authoritative sources of all kinds of information about benefits. Other companies operate in the equally valid belief that all employees should have access to such information from a central source located in the personnel office. Most companies operate somewhere between these two approaches.

Procedure to Determine Objectives

The following five-step procedure can help you determine objectives for communicating information about benefits to your employees.

1. Define current or expected problems caused by inadequate awareness of the value of benefits or insufficient knowledge of plan provisions.
2. Rank these problems in order of importance, and group them under headings like Attitude or Appreciation, and Awareness of Information Lack.
3. Identify specific employee groups by age, rank, location, and other factors according to their need for information or for attitude improvement.
4. Identify areas of concern that could influence a potential communication effort, such as the particular requirements of minority groups, the organization's community image, the amount of technical knowledge required for pension computing, possible future changes in plans resulting from labor negotiations, and so on.
5. Establish requirements for catch-up communication with new employees.

These points will now be discussed in greater detail.

Step 1: Defining problems. This step may at first seem to be the least productive, but it might well yield the greatest input. The first task is to meet with those concerned with benefits planning. What's ahead for the future? What is likely to be added in negotiations? How much?

Some questions should also be posed to those directly concerned with benefits administration. Which aspects of the program do employees ask about most frequently? Which do they comment on? What information do they now have that they don't seem to need?

Next, perhaps, should be a sampling of employees themselves. To what extent are they aware of their benefits? Are they a source of pride? What don't employees understand about the benefits? What is their estimate of their value?

A final thought: What would be the consequences of not changing current communication activities?

Step 2: Ranking problems. In assembling the results of Step 1 under two headings, Attitudes and Awareness, an order of importance should suggest itself. Employment trends may govern it. Is the company attempting to hire greater numbers of technically competent white-collar employees? Are wage scales changing? Is a need developing for increased employee mobility between plant locations? Is the union exerting pressure for new benefits? Is the company growing internationally?

Step 3: Identifying employee groups. The differing informational needs and views of various groups of employees will have become apparent during Step 1. At this point, it is necessary to identify carefully the differences and their relative importance in terms of the effects of communications about benefits.

Some judgments can now be made about the views gleaned during Step 1. To what extent do you want employees to be educated about the details of your plans? How much do they need to know about their benefits, and how much do they want to know?

Similar questions can be posed for each group as the results become apparent. To what extent should each depend on staff counselors? Ideally, what should the attitudes of each group be?

Step 4: Identifying areas of concern. Many of the answers in this step will come from your own experience and observations. Discussion with other employers in the community may help confirm your assessment. Educators and your own training people may also be able to make useful contributions.

The purpose of Step 4 is to determine, at least in general terms, what your audience is thinking about. Obviously they will react to your proposed communication, but how? Identifying their reactions is an important phase of the communication process and can prevent wasted effort and expense.

If you expect a negative or critical response from some groups, you will need to set up a process whereby comments and complaints can be channeled and answered correctly and positively. Without this sort of planning, the value of the communication effort can be lost. With it, the positive aspects can be reinforced, and the employee's negative attitudes can be turned into positive responses. Response systems can be built into benefits communication programs in a number of ways, and these are examined in Chapter 5.

Step 5: Establishing requirements for new employees. The amount of communication needed with new employees can readily be assessed as part of the objective-setting process. When should the communication process begin—on the day the employee is hired, or after he has been on the job a month? How much does he need to know? What will his reference needs be? Also, to what extent should you encourage employees to enroll in contributory plans?

All these questions, if not considered at the outset, normally arise in the course of planning or executing a communications program. Once committed to a course of action, however, you will not always find it easy or economical to adjust to changing conditions or new circumstances. Anticipating such developments in advance can enhance the potential effectiveness of any effort, communication or otherwise.

On the basis of this assembled knowledge, the determination of concrete objectives becomes a more logical exercise. If you haven't already done so, you should at this stage check to be sure that all communications are closely aligned with corporate objectives regarding personnel. Does the company want to demonstrate that it is truly concerned with the welfare of its employees? Does it consider benefits an integral and valuable part of the entire compensation program? Perhaps your company is guided by a combination of these objectives and others. Recognizing them at the outset will insure that your communciations about benefits are consistent with overall policy and intent.

Significance of Past Activity

Another important question to answer is: What has been done in the past? For example, has any effort been made to tailor benefits communications to the specific interests of particular employee groups? If so, what has been the response? Has any study been made of the information needs of employees' families? How do college placement directors react to your communications?

We might call all this intelligence information. Its importance may be emphasized by citing the experience of one American company which planned its approach to communicating information about benefits for a subsidiary in Puerto Rico. The basic objective was to win employee support for a new basic and major medical insurance plan modeled on the company's domestic plan.

Uncertain of the interests of its Puerto Rican employees, the company nevertheless made three initial assumptions—that employees would show almost automatic interest in an American-type plan, that they would be reluctant to lose their current access to the free clinics, and that they would show some antagonism when asked to meet the higher cost of the new plan.

An early check of the employees' attitudes quickly altered these assumptions. Intelligence showed that employees and their families were dissatisfied with the company's existing medical plan and the clinics program, that they would prefer the additional coverage the new plan offered, and that they were willing to pay for it. They accorded no particular prestige to an American-type plan—nor did they have any particular interest in it.

Communication objectives were then revised to stress the improved benefits the new plan offered, its responsiveness to a variety of problems, and the freedom of choice it offered participants. Additional emphasis was placed on the value of the new plan despite the higher cost involved.

Quantitative Goals

By this stage you should have a good idea of the environment in which you will be communicating. You will have identified specific audiences, ranging from the senior executive group through all ranks of employees to those outside the organization who will be on the receiving end, such as college placement officers and potential employees in the community workforce. You will also have formed a better idea of the most effective times to communicate, and will have developed a better understanding of the content of your communications in terms of meeting, reinforcing, and changing current attitudes where necessary.

Now, what about defining the objectives themselves?

And what about the quantitative objectives discussed earlier in this chapter?

These will vary according to how the general objectives are to be achieved, and whether they should be attained over a short or long period of time. For example, a quantitative goal might require that sufficient understanding of available survivorship options be established over a five-year period so that the number of employees eligible to elect them grows from 30 to 60 percent. Another might be to double the number of employees subscribing to a savings program. Yet another might be to cut in half the number of inquiries about benefits directed at the personnel office by increasing the knowledge of supervisors in that area. An alternate plan, which is no less valid in other circumstances and with another group of employees, might be to reduce by half the questions posed to supervisors in favor of faster, more authoritative information from a central counseling source. The objective for launching a new plan might well be to communicate its advantages effectively enough to insure a 90 percent enrollment.

Objectives, like departmental budgets, should be both specific and reasonably attainable. The results of the step-by-step intelligence gathering should help establish these goals. If you have any doubts about them, test your communication with a small group of employees. Initial reactions are often quite valid in samplings of this kind.

Sample Objectives

Here are some sample objectives in brief:

1. Motivate optimum performance.
2. Build satisfaction and loyalty.
3. Improve on-the-job relationships between employees and management.

4. Lower employee turnover.
5. Increase support of the company by employees' families.
6. Maintain the image of corporate social responsibility.
7. Attract good job applicants.

Here are some more detailed objectives.

Maintain a continuous corporate communications program about benefits that

- Builds employee understanding of all benefits and the various provisions of the plans.
- Enhances employee knowledge of how to obtain maximum value from the available benefits.
- Increases employee appreciation of the total benefits program and all its components.
- Obtains employee cooperation in controlling medical claims.

Two Important Steps

Once your objectives are drafted, two important steps must be taken. The first is to obtain the approval and support of senior management. This step must be carried out before any communications program is launched. Some aspects of the program will require the participation of top management, often involving letters to staff, canvassing senior supervisors, and launching meeting sessions, to say nothing of budget approval.

The second step is to make sure that all other members of management are aware of the objectives and are prepared to back them up. If a manager is helping to attain a series of objectives which he has been asked to consider and approve in the developmental stages, he is hardly likely to refuse to participate. He may even provide some useful and imaginative input of his own to boost the program. If the program answers questions that have been bothering him personally, he will soon appreciate the need to be able to answer queries himself.

Distributing copies of objectives to other line managers and supervisors is another prudent technique that can pay valuable dividends. Supervisors are generally in a powerful position to help employees increase their appreciation of the value of benefits. Knowledge of the objectives can make them feel more involved in the total program.

3

Planning the Program

THE amount of effort required to draw up a set of objectives will provide a good indication of the scope of the actual communications task at hand. The size of the audience and the needs of its individual members will make one point clear: Sporadic, unplanned communications cannot be expected to have lasting results. However well conceived and executed, their effect will be at best a hit-and-miss matter.

You will learn the variety of information needs of the audience and the social climate of parts of the organization through discussion with both management and rank-and-file employees. Perhaps their comments will provide pertinent information on the effectiveness of previous communication efforts and will give you insight that will help you formulate your messages.

The form of any communication plan is strongly influenced by the human setting in which it is to take place. Specific plans, techniques, and messages must be designed to achieve clearly defined goals for specific audiences.

Choosing Tactics

To achieve your objectives, you might have to use various sets of communication tactics, depending on what your intelligence homework tells you about each audience. For example, in a program to win employees' acceptance of a new contributory thrift plan that replaces a noncontributory profit-sharing plan, these tactics might be used:

If Audience Is	Use These Tactics
Highly educated	Tell both sides of story (values and drawbacks)
Potentially hostile toward new plan	Supply detailed data plus many interpretations
Mobile	Stress rapid growth, early vesting, and so on
At family peak	Stress death benefits and withdrawal rights
In the high-income category	Stress voluntary contribution and tax advantages

For an audience with other characteristics, an alternative set of tactics should be used:

If Audience Is	Use These Tactics
Poorly educated	Lean toward one side of story
Potentially favorable toward new plan	Supply highlight data with minimum of detailed interpretation
Not mobile	Stress long-range growth of savings
Past family peak	Stress disability and retirement income values
In the lower-income category	Stress company-match (light-touch voluntary contributions)

Thus, the tactics you choose clearly depend on the results of your intelligence homework in identifying the characteristics of various employee audiences. An obvious breakdown would separate salaried from hourly employees, executive and management from general salaried personnel, and union from nonunion hourly employees.

Pitfalls of Simple Programs

An important distinction will need to be made if some employees are covered by plans carried over from companies absorbed through merger or acquisition. Complications may arise if people transferred to the parent company at the time of merger have since been relocated or promoted to groups where they can no longer be regarded as a unit of audience.

Different challenges and opportunities will be posed by employee groups covered by contributory plans, as opposed to any employees in the same general audience who are not required to contribute at all. What might at first appear to be an easy communication situation can contain as many potential pitfalls as the more difficult task of communicating information about increases in employee contributions or reductions in benefit levels. One example would be the matter of introducing a completely new plan to a group not currently covered by contributory plans. Experience in introducing new plans has shown that they often evoke less response than they deserve. The primary reason for this is that the impact of launching a new plan is expected in itself to create considerable appreciation; in fact, however, an unplanned, ill-considered introduction can easily produce feelings of suspicion and criticism among unprepared employees.

Basic Questions

One key source of the necessary background information for determining audience characteristics will be administrators of benefits and others in the personnel function who have day-to-day contact with employees. Their responses can be amplified by further discussion with supervisors, with employees known to be thought leaders, and, perhaps, with union officials.

Senior executives in charge of large departments, such as manufacturing and sales, will also be able to contribute valuable comments to the communications planner. These executives will have assessed the value of various plans in helping to attract new employees, and will know from the comments of retiring employees which benefits are appreciated most and which least.

Trends and attitudes identified in earlier interviews can be usefully employed to guide these discussions. For instance, if early interviews indicate that many employees consider the pension plan to be inadequate, later meetings should be designed to determine whether that attitude does indeed exist, and, if so, to learn why. The interviewer should prepare himself as thoroughly for these discussions as he would for any other important business meeting.

Checking with Supporters and Critics

An organization with widespread operations may find it desirable to conduct sample interviews at selected locations. These should include not only sites where employee dissent might be expected, but also an equal representation of views from locations where a high degree of appreciation exists.

The meetings with informal thought leaders among

general employee groups will yield patterns of information and views which will be corroborated and amplified by personal interviews with supervisors and executives. Before all the data are transcribed in report form, the patterns calling for correction or reinforcement of the communication techniques will become clear. Closer analysis, together with careful development of specific tactics, will then be required.

As the study progresses, the company may decide to eliminate some of the planned interviews or, alternatively, to add other locations to the schedule, or to do both. Companies which follow this pattern find that they need to adjust the number of interviews as the interviews themselves progress, to increase the number of meetings held in locations where consistent patterns have not developed, or to decrease them in areas where patterns are clearly established.

This process, or exercise, will help the planner become aware of the range of problems he must overcome if he is to devise an effective communications program. These problems can be just as numerous in a small company as in a large one, and may require quite a different set of tactics to overcome.

The informal interviews should include both some younger employees and some longer-service personnel, whose needs for communications about benefits will differ as much as will those of newly hired employees. And, of course, at least one planned question for each executive interviewed should be: What is your personal attitude toward the benefits program, and toward the frequency, content, and value of the communications you are currently receiving?

Incidentally, these questions may well yield replies quite similar to the views the executive has already expressed about employee attitudes and needs. If this is so, or even if the two sets of comments are in conflict, the comparison or conflict will in itself invite further questions from the researcher.

Analyzing the Findings

The next phase in the intelligence process is to analyze the findings in detail, tabulating attitudes and needs by levels, locations, and patterns that indicate where correction is necessary. What may evolve is a common need for certain information throughout the organization, and various other information needs according to location or employee group. Whatever the results, it is certain that the company which ignores any aspects calling for correction will inevitably impair the effectiveness of the principal announcement or program to be communicated.

The survey process outlined above is suggested as the minimum necessary basis for developing any effective tactics for communicating. The value of thorough attitude surveys to provide more accurate and in-depth measurement of attitudes and awareness is discussed in Chapter 5.

Short- and Long-term Plans

The results of a series of interviews, however few or many, will inevitably yield a large quantity of comment and information. The first task of the interviewer is to list categories and groups of employees in terms of their information needs and desires. Observations about their attitudes should accompany each grouping. These data will be of considerable assistance in the next phase of the exercise—assigning short- and long-term priorities to their needs.

The identification of these priorities will depend largely

on the character of the immediate activity. For example, significant changes are being made in one or more benefit plans, or if an entirely new plan is being introduced, the immediate need will be to communicate details of the new provisions.

The intelligence survey may also indicate that the time is opportune for a complete, in-depth review with all employees of all benefits, statutory as well as corporate.

For the longer term, the interviews may indicate a need for continuing reinforcement among all employees—or certain segments—of the value of all their benefits. This sort of reinforcement may be confined only to highlights. The form can be determined later; what is important at this stage is to know what the immediate needs are, and to what extent and how often employees in all categories should be reminded of their benefits.

Many of the decisions to be made at this point center on the timeliness of communicating information about new as well as existing or changed benefits. The effective dates of the benefit plans may have some bearing, but the most influential factors will be the possible effect on approaching negotiations, company competitiveness within the industry, and the need for coordination with other current communications activity within the company.

Budgeting for Results

The need for budgets in planning a communications program is as valid as for any other ongoing business operation. Obviously, funds must be available for work that is anticipated in the future, and budgeting is part of the planning exercise that provides the necessary assurance.

Budgeting for communications, however, often falls short of doing an adequate job because of undue emphasis on short-term needs. A typical example is the earmarking of funds to issue a new booklet about plans at the time changes in them are contemplated, but without considering the ongoing work necessary to keep alive in employees' minds the highlights of the new provisions, let alone the value of the total plan, on a continuing basis.

Setting budget targets for continuing communications about all plans over a two- or three-year period is no more difficult than forecasting the costs of communicating information about changes in plans. Staff time must be considered, whether or not required in the formal corporate budgeting process. Out-of-pocket costs for announcements, posters, folders, and possibly meeting locations can be anticipated with a fair degree of accuracy. Downtime costs for employees to attend meetings during company hours may or may not be a formal budget requirement. Even if it is not, it may be interesting to work it out as part of the real cost of communicating.

Longer-term budgeting has two principal advantages. First, it enables the costs of launching new programs and producing expensive material like ring binders to be amortized to some extent over more than one year. Second, it spares the responsible communicator from having to seek approval every time he wants to set up meetings or produce materials that are part of the continuing communication process.

How Much to Spend

One of the best ways of establishing a ceiling on your communication expenses is to estimate the possible costs of not communicating at all.

Employees who are unaware that they have any benefits are not going to be around very long; a number of them will quit to work elsewhere. Many of these will be members of management and consequently expensive to replace. Those who stay are inevitably going to worry about their own and their families' security in time of illness and disability, and their fears will affect their own ability to work and contribute effectively. Senior employees who are not aware of any pension benefits are undoubtedly going to become more apprehensive about meeting the cost of living in retirement, and their job efficiency can be expected to decline.

The costs of not communicating can thus be developed as extensively as the imagination will allow. What, then, of the cost of communicating effectively? Is there a valid yardstick?

One meaningful technique is to relate the communication budget to the cost of the benefits themselves. This approach has two main features. First, it provides a logical way of relating communication costs to the value of the subject matter to be communicated. It is not unlike the way manufacturers relate advertising and promotion expenses to the costs of production. Perhaps more significantly, this approach is a useful way to demonstrate to management just how little needs to be spent to communicate information about benefits.

Second, a very small fraction of the annual cost of the benefits themselves usually provides a more than ample communications budget. For example, a company with benefits costing $3 million a year could budget $25,000 for communications purposes and still be spending less than 1 percent of its benefits expenditure.

Standard or Deluxe?

Presenting information about benefits to an employee requires an approach different from that used to decide about lunchroom décor or the carpeting in managers' offices. Unlike products and working environment, benefits cannot be seen and touched. They are essentially a promise. Nevertheless, they are an expensive promise, both to design and to provide, and management's pride in the quality of its promise should be reflected in the way it is packaged.

"Packaging" in this sense means not only the appearance of the communication materials, but also the messages they contain. Multilithed material stapled in a file folder can be just as effective in a small company as an industrial giant's four-color, glossy-papered manual—provided the wording is meaningful, understandable, and believable. The office copier edition of a booklet can in fact be infinitely more effective if it meets the employee's information needs better than more elaborate publications. In other words, it is preferable to produce a simple device well than to offer an obviously expensive medium that doesn't begin to do an adequate job of communicating.

For those who are in doubt about the extent to which they should commit themselves to printing work, the effort to consult a series of design consultants or printers—which may be necessary in any case to obtain competitive bids—may well yield a variety of production ideas and alternatives that offer pleasing results.

Regardless of the communication medium you choose, the cost of writing and art direction will depend on the sources you use. If these jobs are done by your own company staff, their salary and time will determine the cost. If outside sources are used, fees will depend mainly on the amount and complexity of the information you want to communicate.

One cost pitfall to be wary of in the production process is author's alterations, as they are classified in printers' invoices. These are charges for changes made in text after the type has been set. Charges for typesetting normally amount to at least half the total printing cost, and any changes in proofs other than necessary corrections can result in expenses that boost the final printing bill by as much as 20 or 30 percent above the original estimate. Be sure that all changes and approvals are made before the typewritten draft and art layout are submitted for production.

A Final Word

Quality is a vital consideration in the budgeting process. Shoddy-looking material that is difficult to understand is, in effect, telling employees that you don't care much about them or the effectiveness of the benefits program. Also, confusing information may do more harm than good by creating more problems than it resolves.

As John Ruskin is reported to have said: "It's unwise to pay too much, but worse to pay too little. When you pay too much you lose a little money, but that's all. When you pay too little, you sometimes lose everything, because the thing you buy is incapable of doing the thing it was bought to do."

This is not meant to imply that the only other alternative is not to communicate at all. Silence achieves nothing. The point is that you should spend what you can to communicate often and well.

4

The Tools of the Trade

THE breakthroughs in media technology which occurred during the 1960s have had far-reaching effects on communications. Computers now spit out in seconds data which used to take months or more to compile. Projectors which once had to be carried by two men and a boy now collapse into neat briefcase-size packages. It is even possible to produce and show your own color television programs with equipment that retails for as little as the price of a couple of electric typewriters.

Such devices have vastly expanded the capabilities of the person planning a benefits communications program. But they also pose a very real hazard, because it is quite easy to become preoccupied with the gadgetry at the expense of the message you are trying to communicate.

Possibly nothing written by an American is better remembered than the Gettysburg Address. Yet Lincoln wrote it on the back of an envelope and delivered it without the help of a TelePrompTer or public address system, and he used no visual aids. People remember it because it was beautifully written, meaningful to the audience, and entirely appropriate to the occasion.

This is not to say that media selection isn't important. It is. Sometimes a creative choice of media not only can increase the impact of the message you are communicating, but can also result in cost savings.

Take group meetings, for instance. Because such meetings are usually conducted during business hours, they tend to be expensive. In addition to having to pay employees to attend, you must consider the downtime expense of lost profit, interrupted work schedules, travel time to and from the meeting site, and other costs. In a service business, downtime costs may range anywhere from a multiple of one-half to two or three times compensation or even more. In a manufacturing organization, they may be considerably higher.

As an alternative to group meetings, a few companies have, under selected circumstances, turned to the medium of open-circuit television on commercial or educational channels. With employees viewing the telecasts on their own time—evenings or weekends—the economic advantages can be substantial. For example, assuming average compensation of $4 an hour and a downtime factor of two, the cost of having 5,000 people attend a half-hour meeting works out to $20,000 ($4 $\times$ 2 $\times$ 5,000 / 2). Opposed to this is the cost of one-half hour of air time, which might amount to less than $2,000 in medium-size markets like Atlanta, Milwaukee, or San Francisco.

The cost of producing a television program could eat up any savings, of course. But it doesn't have to, according to at least one company. Production costs for its own program amounted to no more than the amount that would have been spent on materials and arrangements for group meetings.

Factors in Media Selection

Of course, the choice of media to communicate about benefits will hinge on a number of factors other than the pros and cons peculiar to each. Here are some of them.

Objectives. Is the purpose of your communication to educate employees about the specific provisions and workings of their benefits, or to build an overall appreciation of them? Is your goal to motivate employees to some specific action, such as enrolling in a plan? Or is it all of these, some combination of them, or something else entirely?

Audience. How large a group are you attempting to reach? How is it composed with respect to age, sex, educational level, employment status, or other categories? Is the entire group in one location or is it scattered?

Equipment, facilities, and manpower. If you are planning to conduct group meetings, are adequate meeting rooms available? Do you have the necessary audiovisual equipment or can it be rented? Do you have people with the time and skills required to run the meetings, or will they have to be trained? If so, for how long and by whom?

Message. How long and how complex a story are you planning to tell? Would it be better to break it into bits and pieces, or can you do it all at once? Is it likely to provoke a positive or negative response?

Timing. Must everyone get the story at approximately the same time, or can you spread the effort out over a period of weeks or months? How much lead time do you have for planning, writing, and production?

Money. How much can you afford to spend for materials, for outside help, for staff time of people working on the project, and for the downtime costs of those to whom you are communicating?

The answers to questions like these will not only provide a guide to the medium or combination of media best suited to accomplish your objectives, but, in many cases, will make the choice obvious.

Two Types of Media

Two basic types of media are used to communicate benefits information: those which transmit information in a downward direction from management to employees, and those which carry information upward from employees to management. Downward communications media are normally used for one or more of these five purposes:

1. To announce an addition to or a change in a benefit plan or program.
2. To provide a reference source of information about benefits.
3. To provide depth education about certain aspects of a benefit plan or program.
4. To remind employees of the existence and value of their benefits.
5. To assist employees with their personal planning.

Upward communications media, on the other hand, are generally employed to accomplish one or more of these three goals:

1. To assess employees' attitudes and opinions about benefits.
2. To determine employees' level of knowledge about benefits.
3. To create a benchmark so that it is possible to measure the effectiveness of future communications efforts.

The balance of this chapter discusses those media with

which the benefits communicator is most likely to become involved. The only omissions are formal surveys of attitudes, opinions, and knowledge, since these are treated at length in the next chapter. Also, the term "media" is used somewhat loosely here, since the following discussion includes various devices which, while not media in the strictest sense of the word, are close enough in usage to be classified as such. Finally, the reader should not assume that there is a relationship between the length of the description and the value or importance of the medium.

Advisory Councils

In an effort to promote better upward communication, many companies have established advisory councils composed of employees who are either appointed by management or elected by their associates. Terms usually run for at least a year.

Council members are charged with the responsibility of reflecting the ideas and feelings of their fellow employees. Although agenda topics may span the spectrum of corporate operations, both the structure and administration of the employee benefit program are frequently discussed. Consequently, these councils can provide valuable input for the benefits communicator.

Announcement Folders

These are succinctly worded pieces, usually four to six pages long, designed to highlight changes in a benefit plan or program, or to outline the more important provisions of a newly adopted plan. Usually distributed at the close of group meetings on the same subject, the folders serve to reinforce the message that was presented orally. In addition, since it may not be practical to have booklets published by the time the meetings are held, the announcement folder can also double as an interim reference document. (See Figure 1.)

Figure 1. Announcement Folder, Reynolds

Announcement Letters

The announcement letter is simply a vehicle for notifying employees of a forthcoming change. If the change is minor or easily understood, such as an across-the-board increase in the amount of noncontributory group life insurance, the letter alone may suffice until a revised booklet can be issued. If the change is complex or extensive, however, some additional form of communication, such as group meetings, will probably be planned. In that case, the less said in the letter, the better. Ideally, it would state only the effective date of the change, the fact that the recipient will be invited to attend a group meeting where full information will be presented, and any reassurances that can be given (for example, "No one's benefits will be reduced" or "There will be no increase in your contributions"). Even if the letter is very carefully worded, telling more than necessary can result in rumors or misunderstandings which may be very difficult to correct.

Booklets

Booklets come in all shapes, sizes, art styles, and copy approaches, and they may be printed in one, two, three, four, or more colors. In other words, they can be as simple or elaborate as taste, budget, and other circumstances warrant. But no matter what they look like or how much they cost, they should pass three tests—accuracy, completeness, and readability. And this is no small order. Most booklets are accurate and reasonably complete, but many of them suffer from a bad case of legalese. The only known cure is writing talent.

In developing a written description of a benefits program, it is possible to go in one of three directions. You can describe all plans in your program in one booklet, or you can print a separate booklet for each plan, or you can cover all plans in a looseleaf binder.

The first approach is usually the least expensive initially, since you need print only one cover, one table of contents, and so on. But when a revision is necessary, you must reprint the entire booklet. Even in situations where changes are not foreseen for some time (for example, when benefits are negotiated under long-term contracts), you must still contend with the possibility of changes in Social Security and other statutory benefits.

The second approach mitigates the revision problem since you need reprint fewer pages when a change occurs. However, several booklets generally cost more to begin with than does a single booklet covering the same benefits. Also, most companies which use this approach enclose the booklets in some sort of packet, which also costs money.

A looseleaf binder represents the last word in economical updating, since it can be revised by reprinting only those pages which are affected by the change. But again, the initial cost is usually greater than either of the two other approaches, since vinyl or board covers and rings are more expensive than paper and staples.

Although all three approaches are popular, more and more companies seem to be producing looseleaf binders, as much for esthetic reasons as for ease of updating. Those that don't, frequently claim that some employees won't take the trouble to insert revised pages. This is undoubtedly true, but you must wonder whether these aren't the same people who can't find their booklets when they want them anyway.

Bulletin Boards

Bulletin boards can be used to best advantage to attract attention and to create anticipation; hence, they are good for announcements. They are not suited for communication of detailed messages because of space limitations and because employees lack sufficient time to read them on the job. If the message is kept short and to the point, maximum impact is achieved.

Although management cannot be certain of reaching all employees through this medium, bulletin boards used consistently to transmit messages of importance can generate a high degree of employee interest and credibility. Attractive posters and notices can usually be produced at relatively low cost.

Certificates of Membership

"This certifies that John Jones is a member in good standing of the XYZ Corporation Retirement Income Plan and, as such, is entitled to all benefits, rights, and privileges it provides, as specified in the official plan document." Such meaningless wording is typical of that used on certificates of membership issued by many companies. Of absolutely no legal consequence, the certificates are usually printed in a diploma format on parchmentlike paper, and are complete with scrolls, seals, and ribbons. Some employees treasure them; others throw them out at the first opportunity.

Claim Check Enclosures

This is an inexpensive yet effective device used by employers who self-insure their medical benefits or who operate medical plans under a draft book system. Enclosing claim checks in folders or envelopes which are imprinted with an appropriate message insures that the message reaches the employee when he is in a particularly positive frame of mind.

Contests

Benefits contests offer an opportunity to inject a bit of fun and friendly competition into what can be a somewhat pedestrian subject. Depending on the way they are designed, contests can serve as downward communication vehicles or as feedback mechanisms. Many formats are possible—essays, writing the caption for a cartoon, guessing the annual expenditure for benefits, to name a few. One employer even ran a beauty contest using the theme "The Girl I'd Most Like to Retire With."

Displays

When placed in high-traffic areas, such as lobbies, cafeterias, and lounges, displays can be an effective medium for reminding employees about the value and workings of their benefits. Displays may be composed only of printed materials, such as posters, photos, and charts. But greater interest can be generated by making use of self-contained audiovisual media. Tape-recorded messages played through earphones, self-repeating rear-screen projections of movies or slides, and electronic question-and-answer boards are just a few of the possibilities.

By installing a Benefits Information Center display near the entrance of his department, one benefits manager accomplished a dual purpose. The display, stocked with copies of booklets, enrollment forms, and other benefit literature, plus blow-ups of the answers to frequently asked questions, reminded all who saw it of the program. It also sharply reduced the number of requests for materials and information received by his staff.

Annual Reports

In recent years, more and more companies have recognized the value of publishing annual reports for employees, just as they do for shareholders. Because such reports are specifically geared to employee interests, it would be hard to imagine one that did not include benefits information. The subject matter frequently covers the financial condition of retirement and profit-sharing funds, group life and medical insurance claims, disability payments, enrollment statistics, and corporate and employee expenditures for benefits, as well as summaries of plans which were adopted during the year and changes which were made in existing plans.

In presenting financial information, it is well to remember that many people are not terribly impressed by large numbers per se. Having just read a newspaper that reported a defense contract in the hundreds of millions and a national debt in the billions, a $700,000 contribution to the retirement plan may seem rather measly. However, by interpreting financial information in terms the employee can understand, you can make it meaningful. If, for example, you can say that it would take the profit from the entire production of the Duluth plant to pay for the medical plan or that the company's expenditure for benefits exceeded total dividends paid to shareholders, you stand a better chance of getting through.

Employee Publications

Employee publications can be utilized to announce and interpret changes in benefits, and they can play an important role in maintaining continuing awareness and understanding of the total benefits package. Continuing series of articles can make a significant contribution to employee knowledge. Some companies favor a regular question-and-answer column dealing with specific points posed by employees or taken from the records of inquiries at the personnel office.

Some editors believe a more effective technique is to prepare articles on estate and retirement planning, and to aim them at employees in different age groups. These certainly offer an excellent opportunity to stress company-provided benefits, in terms of both availability and value. Examples of individual cases can be pictured and explained, using actual employees rather than hypothetical situations. Most editors are pleased to carry this type of article, since readership surveys invariably reflect a higher than usual degree of interest in them, from wives and husbands as well as from employees themselves.

Flip Charts

Since it is pretty well established that people retain far more of what they see *and* hear than of what they only hear, most benefits communicators use some sort of visual aids when making verbal presentations. The flip chart is one of the best. In contrast with those media which are projected on a screen, these charts have several advantages. First, there's a lot less chance of equipment failure since there are no bulbs to burn out or mechanisms to go out of whack. Second, it's less awkward to go back to a prior chart (when answering a question, for example) than to roll back a filmstrip or try to find a slide. Finally, because you don't turn out the lights, you run less risk of having a part of your audience slip out a side exit, mentally or physically. (See Figure 2.)

Figure 2. Flip Chart, Monsanto

An important disadvantage is that more training is usually required to make a smooth flip-chart presentation than to make a comparable presentation using slides or a filmstrip. With charts, the entire presentation must be "live," whereas with film the narration can be recorded, leaving the meeting leader only to introduce the subject, run the projector, and handle questions and answers. Even when a completely live film presentation is made, it is much less awkward to use notes since the lights are out and the audience's attention is directed toward the image on the screen, rather than toward the leader. The amount of time needed to train a group of people to make an effective flip-chart presentation will depend on the length of the presentation, the group's familiarity with the subject matter, and the leadership skills of the persons who are being trained. In general, it's well to allow two to three days to train a group of inexperienced people to make a 45-minute to one-hour presentation about an unfamiliar subject, such as a new benefit plan.

Flip charts may be produced in virtually any size. Standard dimensions for those intended for use in meetings of 20 to 25 employees are 30 inches wide by 40 inches long. Copy is best limited to about 30 characters per line and to no more than eight or nine lines per chart. Liberties may be taken with these specifications when presenting tabular or graphic information.

Flip charts may be more or less expensive to produce than slides or filmstrips, depending on the number of sets needed. Other things being equal, the cost of silk-screened charts reduces less as the quantity increases than does the cost of additional sets of slides or filmstrip prints.

Because anyone who can write can make flip charts, there's a great temptation to save time and money by making them yourself. But unless you've majored in calligraphy or have real lettering skills, it's better not to. Homemade charts always look amateurish. And in using them, you run the risk of having the audience infer a correlation between the quality of the benefits you are describing and the materials you are using to describe them. If the budget just won't stand the cost of professionally prepared charts, use chalk and blackboard to make your presentation.

Group Meetings

If today's hippie communes are a valid indicator that our industrial society is not providing enough personal and physical contact, then the value of group meetings, which have long been considered among the most productive of communication devices, will be enhanced even more in the future. The principal advantage of the group meeting is that the employee has an opportunity to hear at first hand a verbal interpretation of plans and programs that affect him, and can ask questions and have them answered to his satisfaction. In the case of meetings conducted by supervisors, a secondary advantage is the opportunity for them to become known to employees as primary, reliable sources of information.

Following are some basic guides for conducting effective group meetings.

Group size. Attendance at any one meeting should not exceed 20 to 25 employees. If groups are much larger, two-way discussion tends to be more difficult and the upward communication value of the meetings is thereby reduced.

Meeting place. Wherever possible, meetings should be held in quiet and private locations. Meeting rooms should be equipped with conference tables and, as required, with visual-aid equipment such as easels and charts, blackboards, projectors, and screens.

Meeting leadership. The effectiveness of meetings depends greatly upon the leader's ability. Conference leadership requires skill in effective presentation; moreover, it requires an ability to stimulate and guide employee participation. These skills and abilities can be acquired through proper training.

To help insure prompt and adequate upward communication to management, a program of standardized feedback reports from leaders is useful. For each meeting he conducts, the leader's report form should summarize the following information.

- Date of the meeting.
- Employee reactions to subject matter.
- Employee complaints and suggestions.
- Questions asked by employees and the answers that were given.
- Unanswered questions requiring later follow-up.

Formalized group meetings should not preclude tailgate or work-place meetings that supervisors may conduct periodically. Some companies provide subject outlines to stimulate such sessions. One organization issued first-line supervisors a series of 26 three- to five-minute talks covering various aspects of its benefits program. These were delivered every two weeks during coffee breaks over a period of a year.

Letters

Letters to the home are economical and fast to produce and distribute. When the subject matter touches the employee's pocketbook—as benefit topics usually do—the letters are well read, by both the employee and his spouse. These letters may be issued on a regular quarterly or monthly schedule or as the need arises.

Imprinted Items

Matchbook covers, paper cups, memo pads, and cafeteria table tents all may be imprinted with a message or slogan about benefits. They are cheap to produce and useful to supplement other communications efforts.

Medical Membership Cards

Membership cards are issued by many employers as evidence of coverage under a medical insurance plan. While their primary value is in easing admittance to a hospital, they also act as continuing reminders of benefits, since many employees carry them in their wallets. Often a brief summary of benefits is printed on the back of the card.

Movies

Because of their ability to create a mood and generate an emotional response, movies are a unique medium. They are, however, poor devices for transmitting the detailed kind of information which characterizes many benefits communications. Consequently, they are usually reserved for major efforts, such as the launching of a new benefits program, and are used in conjunction with other media which are better suited to convey factual information.

Movies imply entertainment, and this enhances their acceptance by employees at all levels of the organization. They also help communicate with employees who may have difficulty comprehending printed material.

Although production costs are high, movies can often be used for multiple purposes, such as recruitment and employee orientation. Also, trained meeting leaders are not needed each time the movie is screened. Thus, movies offer particular advantages to companies whose employees are widely dispersed geographically.

Newsletters

These are economical and efficient vehicles for communicating benefits information. They do not need to be expensive or elaborate in format or design. A simple masthead can be prepared, issues typed, and copies distributed quickly. Because of its relatively simple production, the newsletter has a definite advantage over many other communications media. If limited to the subject of benefits, a newsletter can be published as needed rather than on a regular basis, like an employee newspaper.

Payroll Inserts

Management opinions about payroll inserts vary widely. Some employers use them regularly; others feel that an employee's pay envelope ought to hold his pay and nothing else. If you do wish to use inserts, they are best suited to simple announcements or reminders.

On the theory that inserts are seen, even if they aren't read, one employer developed an extensive program involving inserts which were color coded to various elements of the benefits package (blue for the retirement plan, red for group insurance, and so on). Since all other communications materials were similarly coded, employees couldn't help but think about benefits when they opened their pay envelopes. Copy for each insert discussed one provision or fact about a specific benefit plan.

Posters

Posters are fast and inexpensive to produce, but good ones are difficult to design. Because readership time may last only a second or two, they must communicate instantly. Thus, it is imperative to keep the message simple and words to a minimum. Ideally, the artwork alone should tell the story.

Benefit posters may be purchased readymade from a

number of organizations, or you can have your own made to order. In either case, you should have enough to be able to change them fairly frequently, once a week, for example.

A final word about posters: Don't expect too much of them. They are fine for purposes such as reminding employees of their benefits in general or asking them to take a specific action, (for example, to sign up for a new plan by a specific date). But they are not suitable for accomplishing broad communications objectives or communicating detailed information.

Programmed Instruction

Although programmed instruction might more properly be viewed as a learning device than as a communications medium, it does have definite application for companies interested in increasing employees' knowledge and understanding of their benefits. It has been widely and successfully used in training circles but its use in communicating employee benefits information has been largely overlooked.

There are, however, a few exceptions. A midwestern food processor successfully used programmed instruction to acquaint company negotiators with the intricacies of pension funding in preparation for bargaining sessions. A large public retirement system developed a program to assist about-to-retire members to make intelligent choices of payment options.

A program may be designed in any one of a number of formats. Booklets, slides, filmstrips, and tape, have all been used. Depending on its construction, a program may be used to teach anything from simple facts to complex concepts and judgment skills.

Writing a program involves four fundamental steps: (1) dividing the knowledge to be imparted into discrete fragments, (2) arranging the fragments in a logical order, (3) calling for specific responses to questions asked, and (4) providing immediate confirmation of the answers. But although writing a program may appear simple, it is not a job for amateurs. Organizations which have effectively used programmed learning stress the need to develop competent internal resources or else to employ professional outside help.

Experts in the field agree that a given segment of instruction should not require more than one hour to complete, although 20 to 30 minutes is definitely preferable. It should be noted, however, that an entire course covering a subject in detail might well require a number of sittings.

Some important advantages of programmed instruction are:

- It's fun. Most employees find the novelty of completing a program a satisfying and enjoyable experience.
- It can be done on the employee's own time and at his own pace.
- It's effective. Because programmed instruction is participative in nature, many people acquire knowledge faster and retain it longer than they do through other means.

Its disadvantages, if they can be considered as such, are that it does require professional help to design, and that it is relatively time-consuming and expensive to produce. A commonly used rule of thumb (but only that) is that you should be prepared to spend about $2,000 for each hour of instruction.

Recordings

Whether they take the form of phonograph records, tape reels, or sound tracks on films, recordings offer an advantage that live presentations can't: They assure you that every member of the audience will hear exactly the same message as every other. This advantage can be particularly important if training time or talent is in short supply or if the subject matter to be discussed is complex. The same is true if you must deal with negative or controversial issues, such as a reduction in benefits or the discontinuance of a plan. A serious problem which companies face in conducting live meetings on such issues is that the meeting leader may oversell or gloss over negative issues.

Recordings also offer advantages over print media, under certain circumstances. One is novelty. A record sent to an employee's home is almost certain to be played. Another is dramatic emphasis. Because you can hear voice inflections as well as sound effects, it is often easier to convey your message.

Records are relatively inexpensive to produce. They are also easy to mail, particularly those made of paper-thin, flexible plastic.

Slides and Filmstrips

These are really one and the same thing—photographs taken on 35-mm film. The only difference is that with slides, the strip of film is cut into individual frames which are mounted in metal, plastic, or cardboard masks. Thus, slides may be considered somewhat more flexible since you can change their sequence or add or delete frames easily. On the other hand, with a filmstrip, you needn't ever worry about the frames being out of order. Filmstrips are also a little less expensive to produce since the individual photographs needn't be cut and mounted.

Presentations may be live, or the slides or filmstrip may be synchronized with a recorded narration on a tape cassette or phonograph record. This is usually done by means of an inaudible beep on the recording which trips the projectors's film advance mechanism.

Both slides and filmstrips are popular visual aids for several reasons. First, the equipment to project them is almost always available. If an employer doesn't have a projector, he can usually rent one with little trouble. Second, they are colorful and communicate well. Finally, given a lens of the right focal length, you can adjust the image to suit any size of meeting room.

In recent years, several important improvements in slide projectors have become available, such as zoom lenses and devices that focus each frame precisely and automatically. Projection techniques have improved, too. Through the use of a variety of reasonably priced devices, you can achieve interesting dramatic and multiple-image effects. The net result is that an already popular and versatile medium is becoming even more so.

Special Events

Rather than wait for a communications opportunity to present itself, why not create your own by setting aside a day or week for a benefits appreciation program. Features might include contests, displays, booths where questions can be answered, and a reopening of enrollments for contributory group insurance plans. One large employer sets aside the same day each year for distribution of statements on benefits. The program focuses on departmental meetings where the statements are distributed and profit-sharing results are related to corporate performance. Free coffee and doughnuts and drawings for door prizes help make the meetings enjoyable.

Statements

The statement is possibly the single most popular printed benefits communications medium, since it is completely personal. (See Figure 3.) The information it contains is for the employee and his family alone.

Ranging from simple one-page highlight reports of major benefits to in-depth reports of all benefits and other compensation elements, statements may include as little or as much information as desired. For example:

Benefit amounts. In the life insurance area, this may mean a statement of the employee's current coverage. In the pension area, it could be a projection of retirement income at age 65.

Integration of benefits. Many benefit plans work together, but are often discussed individually. In the case of total and permanent disability, for instance, short-term disability, medical coverage, profit sharing, accidental dismemberment, long-term disability, retirement income plans, and Social Security could all come to an employee's aid. The statement can show how these plans work together, and the actual dollars the employee would receive from each.

Costs of benefits. Costs are usually an eye opener whether or not the plans are partially contributory. The dollar cost of the benefits—plan by plan and total—can be an impressive figure. If some or all of the plans are contributory, the employee's cost can also be reported.

Retail cost projection. A retail cost comparison of an employee's benefits coverage may be shown on the state-

Figure 3. Employee Benefits Statement, Heublein, Inc.

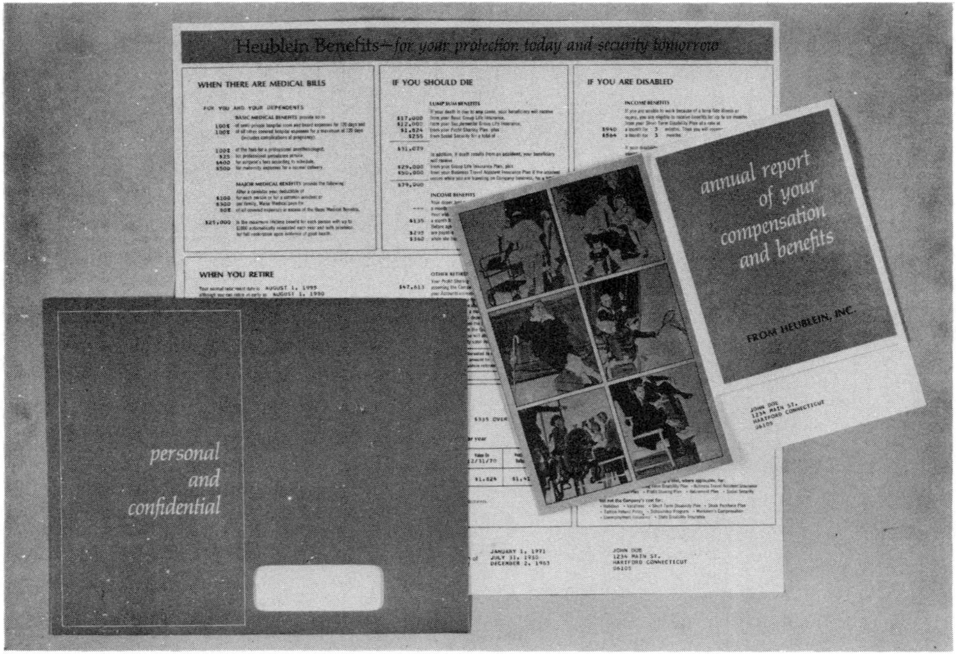

ment. Most employees find this comparison significant, especially when the statement points out the amount of after-tax employee dollars that would have to be paid out for similar private coverage.

Benefits received. The statement can also remind the employee of benefits he has actually received. Although most employees remember the big bills paid by the company's medical plan, they may forget others such as tuition refunds.

A benefits statement can also help communicate many other elements of an employee's total compensation package, including wage and salary breakdowns of earned pay and pay for time not worked (vacations and holidays).

Most of the data for the statement are easily accessible but lie dormant in company computers. And even though computers can do the actual printout of the information, the benefits statement need not be the usual sterile computer form. Tailor-made statements can be designed to help tell an important benefits story in an attractive and colorful setting.

In designing a statement, there are seven steps to follow. These include:

1. Establishing objectives, pinpointing target audiences, and determining the place of the statement in the organization's existing communications program.
2. Determining the benefits and other compensation elements which should be reported on the statement, and the manner in which they should be presented.
3. Coordinating the activities which will be carried out by internal and external resources in order to

produce the statement in the most efficient and economical fashion.
4. Designing and producing the statement forms.
5. Planning and programming the computer to process, validate, and imprint pay and benefits information on the printed form.
6. Distributing the completed forms to employees.
7. Measuring employee response to the statement in order to determine guidelines for future statements.

Most companies that issue statements do so annually. Others produce them semiannually or quarterly.

Open-circuit Television

As discussed earlier in this chapter, open-circuit or commercial television is an intriguing and little explored employee communications medium. In addition to enabling you to communicate with employees on their own time, TV offers these advantages.

You reach the whole family. Television gets through to families of employees as no other medium can. Messages presented at in-plant meetings, if not forgotten, can be misinterpreted by the time employees get home. Through TV, the entire family gets the message at once—and correctly.

TV increases believability. Studies conducted by Elmo Roper indicate that people tend to believe what they see and hear on television more than any other medium of mass communication.

TV is personal. Employees are more likely to be relaxed and receptive to messages they view in their own homes than they might be to presentations they watch in a group meeting. This is especially important to a company that wishes to talk to employees free of the coercive influence of any vocal negative group attitude.

There are also some disadvantages to consider.

TV is public. You can't tune out the general public. Although the primary purpose of the commercial or educational telecast may be to achieve the objectives of communicating information about benefits, the program should also be of interest to the general public. If it can't be done, commercial TV probably isn't the medium for the message.

TV is tentative. A telecast is subject to the whims of programming. One company's program was postponed for nearly an hour because a sports broadcast ran overtime.

TV is sensitive. Errors in timing, tone, and content can be fatal. Mistakes are always magnified on TV.

Companies which have measured reactions to employee-oriented telecasts have found that employee tune-in ranges from 65 to 98 percent.

Closed-circuit Television

Closed-circuit television is defined, technically, as a system of transmitting TV signals to receiving equipment which is directly linked to the originating equipment by coaxial cable, microwave relay, or telephone lines.

Companies that have sponsored closed-circuit telecasts know it can be an extremely expensive medium requiring massive equipment, leased telephone lines, and high-priced technicians. Consequently, it is rarely used to accomplish benefits communications objectives. Today, however, the term "closed circuit" also means internal company TV with inexpensive cameras, monitors, and videotape equipment.

Although this form of closed-circuit TV has been available since the late 1940s, it did not become economically feasible for use by almost any company until 1965. At that time several manufacturers introduced equipment that brought the price of a basic internal closed-circuit system (camera, videotape recorder, and monitor) to between $1,500 and $3,500. This was about one-tenth of the cost of the previous generation of equipment with similar capabilities. Since 1965, a number of advances, such as color capability and improved editing, have made the medium even more attractive.

Although the number of videotape applications for general employee communications objectives is virtually endless, there appear to be two principal ways the medium may be used by the benefits communicator. The first is as a substitute for live group meetings on topics ranging from benefits orientation for new employees to announcement of plan changes. The second is as a training aid to help leaders of meetings to make better presentations. When they are able to see their presentations as the audience would, errors become more apparent to them and are thus more easily corrected.

Transparencies

These are sheets of clear plastic, usually measuring about eight by ten inches, which are prepared to present illustrations or messages and are shown by means of overhead projection. Because of its design, the projector can usually be located only a few feet from the screen, enabling the speaker to remain with it at the front of the meeting room. By pointing or marking directly on the transparency, he can call attention to items of interest.

For formal presentations, it is best to have the transparencies professionally prepared. However, passably good results can be achieved by nonprofessionals using art and lettering kits supplied by a number of organizations. For informal meetings, typewritten copy can be transferred to the film by processing it through office copying machines. Halftones and other graphic effects can also be achieved with special developing equipment. Thus, in a matter of minutes, it is possible to make crude visual aids.

Telephones

Telephones have been used to communicate benefits information in several ways. Larger companies with multiple locations have set up hot-line phone systems when conducting group meetings on new or revised benefits. If a meeting leader is unable to answer an employee's question, he calls the hot-line number and is connected with an expert at headquarters who can. Thus, the meeting leader can quickly get back to the questioner with the right answer.

Dial-a-message phones have also been used on occasion. By dialing a special number, the employee hears a three- or four-minute recorded message. Companies which have used this system suggest changing the message at least once a day to maintain interest. Also, messages about benefits ought to be interspersed with news and other informational items.

5

Measuring the Results

The standard diagrammatic model of the communication process contains two principal figures—the sender and the receiver. The two most important lines of the many that flow between and around them are message and feedback. They are of equal length and equal importance. Around them are other lines and figures representing message coding and decoding, cultural environment, the transmission process, and so on.

The basic figure, however, implies that the feedback process occurs just as spontaneously, strongly, and directly as the sending of the original message. The sender must get a clear and direct feedback or evaluation of how well the message is received and acted upon.

This may be easy enough in situations such as issuing field orders to troops, but it's often difficult to determine how well we are communicating. Most people develop their own systems for evaluating how they are getting through. The comments and responses of those working with you can indicate how well they understand and follow your instructions. Much of the time, however, the accuracy of your feedback is in doubt. At best it may be hazy. Sometimes it is not apparent at all.

The feedback from communicating information about benefits is rarely any more positive. Some employees will ask questions during a meeting or presentation. Most, however, remain silent. Emotional reactions are generally restrained. When employees are offered comparisons with old plans or with the programs of competitors, and are thus in a position to make evaluations, they may react favorably or unfavorably. Whatever the tendency, it is often fairly predictable. But it is never easy to gauge how well you are meeting the generally accepted benefits communication goals of developing understanding and appreciation.

One method of assessing the level of employee understanding of communications is to check the volume and character of questions asked of the personnel office. Another is to determine how frequently employees elect options or choose to participate in contributory plans.

How Honest Are Employees?

Just how much employees actually appreciate their benefits is a question which generally requires more probing. Preretirement training, exit interviews, and counseling on medical disability claims offer regular opportunities to query the recipients of benefits. But how honest are their answers? Are their views representative? Do they appreciate their benefits as added compensation? If so, what value do they place on them?

When survey results are analyzed in terms of various employee classifications, they generally show that younger employees have little interest in longer-range plans like retirement and death benefits, and that higher-rated employees place less value on direct pay than on indirect compensation.

Organizations that audit their communication effort can answer these and related questions with confidence. In so doing, they obtain an indication of how well employees understand the extent and value of their benefits, and to what extent they value those benefits, both as individual plans and as a total program. Additional audits should be conducted whenever changes are introduced in order to assess employee understanding and appreciation of the changes.

Would Employees Contribute More?

Some of the questions an audit can help answer are these:

- How much do employees currently know about their benefits?
- How do they rate the value of these benefits to them?
- How do they view their benefits in relation to those provided by other companies?
- In what ways would they like to see their benefits improved?
- Would they be willing to contribute more for greater or different benefits?
- How frequently would they like to be kept informed about their benefits, and through what media?

Employees at different age levels and with differing family responsibilities can be expected to respond in varying degrees and with varying emphases to these questions. Responses from locations may also be expected to differ from one location to another, since they will reflect local economic and social conditions.

A recent audit by a public utility showed that employee benefits scored high in terms of appreciation and unusually low in terms of pay. The president of the company, in a moment of candor, called the union chairman into his office, showed him the results, and said: "In the next negotiations, we are going to concentrate on pay increases and not touch the benefits."

To his surprise, the union leader answered, "Fine. That's what I've been trying to tell you, but you wouldn't listen."

Flattering Employees

One real advantage of any audit or survey, whether it deals with a single subject area like benefits or seeks views on a variety of topics, is that employees are invariably flattered to know management is interested in their views. When their collective response is tabulated and reported back to them, and action is promised in areas where they expressed a desire for improvement, they invariably believe that their employers are genuinely concerned with their best interests. As a rule, action cannot be promised in every area where employees indicate they would like to see change. But the company can comment on these points, perhaps only to the extent that they require analysis and time to implement. When a company is not in a position to launch a new program, or to improve an existing one, the mere action of taking an audit can satisfy employees of its intention to rectify some of the matters bothering them.

Surveys also have some disadvantages, and the reasons why more organizations do not undertake communication audits or surveys are worth considering. One reason is cost. A thorough, entirely comprehensive survey, using professional assistance in either all or part of it, can be expensive. But there is no reason why a carefully prepared audit of a representative sampling of employees cannot yield results that are nearly as valid and certainly almost as useful as a more comprehensive survey.

Perhaps a more widespread reason for management's unwillingness to embark on surveys of employee understanding and, in particular, opinion, is the fear that the results will reflect unfavorably on their capacity as managers. Another, albeit rare, reason is that some managers believe that a survey of employee opinion is tantamount to an admission that management is unsure of its administrative policies and personnel practices. To the writers' knowledge, neither of these apprehensions has been substantiated in surveys.

Defining Survey Objectives

The primary purpose of any survey of the effectiveness of communications about benefits is to measure the amount of employee knowledge and awareness of all benefits.

Another purpose, with longer-term significance, is to establish the extent of employee satisfaction or dissatisfaction with plan provisions and the general benefits mix. This information can be valuable in considering future modifications and improvements of plans.

Such a survey can also tap employees' feelings regarding the operation of the business, working environment, personnel policies, and quality of supervision. Regardless of the extent of the survey, an important result will be the picture that emerges of the role that benefits, and compensation, play in maintaining employee satisfaction. Identification and eradication of sources of dissatisfaction can lead to development of more positive attitudes.

Three important words that are often associated with surveys of employees are attitude, opinion, and morale. It is important to distinguish among them.

- *Attitude* is usually the accumulation of many experiences, and is the act of evaluating a person, situation, object, or idea in a favorable or unfavorable manner. Attitudes are the sum of a person's likes and dislikes, attractions and repulsions, interests and apathies, or his instinctive feelings on any subject.
- *Opinion* is the expression of these attitudes in words.
- *Morale,* which is more difficult to define, is a group rather than an individual response. Many specialists in survey work claim that morale and job satisfaction are the same thing. The fact that an equal number disagree indicates that the word is open to varying interpretations.

When to Survey

Timing is an important consideration, if only because a mistimed survey can lead to grief and embarrassment. An ideal time is when things are normal. Surveys should not be conducted during the planning stages of major changes, if only because the results may be unfavorably credited to or blamed on the survey. If employees believe that major changes are in the air, survey activity may well convince them that the two efforts are related, and their reponses may well be influenced by undue apprehension, thus destroying their validity.

Other times when surveys should not be done are in the course of adopting new processes or techniques, during periods of widespread pay adjustments or changes in benefit plans, and while union organizing drives or negotiations are in progress. In fact, any indication of impending changes might be considered an inopportune time for surveying.

Basic Approaches

There are two basic techniques for measuring attitudes toward and the effectiveness of communications about benefits. The standardized approach uses carefully phrased questions that elicit employees' attitudes about a particular subject. In the nondirective approach, the employee is asked one or two general questions and then is encouraged to talk as he wishes about the subject under review.

One advantage of the standardized approach is that it poses the same questions to all employees. The questions can focus on particular aspects the organization wishes to explore, and can be designed with the use of a pilot survey —a trial run, in effect—of a sample group. This technique enables the company to make sure that the wording of the questions is interpreted uniformly. Another important advantage of the standardized approach is that responses can be readily coded for keypunching and computer processing in a variety of combinations and employee classifications, ranging from age to work group location.

The nondirective survey, being less structured, requires less preparation. Much of its success as a feedback device, however, depends on the skill of the interviewer in drawing out the views and knowledge of the employee, and in leading him from one topic to another. Often the interviewer in a nondirective survey will use a series of planned questions as an outline so that he can probe deeply into some of the answers given by respondents.

The principal goal of the nondirective approach is to

learn in a more general way what employees are thinking. As a method of auditing attitudes of small groups, or for pilot surveys, it is valuable. But when used with large employee groups, it can pose severe problems of classifying and analyzing results.

A combination of the two approaches is sometimes used, but usually only when questions can be arranged according to employee groups or in locations where definite attitudes are known to prevail on particular subjects.

Collecting the Answers

Choice of an approach leads to the next stage, which is deciding which of several standard methods of data collection to use. The methods are:

- The conventional personal interview.
- The depth interview.
- The mail questionnaire.
- The group-administered questionnaire.

Conventional personal interview. In this situation the interviewer talks with individual employees face to face. He has a set list of questions and rarely deviates from it.

One advantage of this technique is that it involves minimum disruption to employees' normal production work. An honest and satisfactory response can be obtained if the interviewer is skilled in establishing rapport with the employee. On the negative side, the cost of using skilled interviewers to meet individually with employees can be high.

Depth interview. The interviewer deals with employees individually in this technique, too. He has a set list of questions but uses them primarily as a guide so that he can probe deeply into each respondent's answers.

This approach allows the interviewer to explore employee attitudes in sufficient depth to reveal deep-seated desires and needs, and the extent to which they are being satisfied or ignored, in much greater detail than is possible in the one-question-one-answer approach. The depth interview, incorporating as it does the nondirective approach, can be useful in the early stages of questionnaire design when problems of semantics and phrasing are being ironed out.

Mail questionnaire. Mailing a questionnaire to employees' homes is a particularly useful technique if work locations are widely separated. Generally, however, the response is poor. Also, some levels of employees tend to respond more strongly as a group, which tends to lend undue weight to their views.

The advantage of this technique is that replies can be directed to an outside third party, such as a consulting firm that may be involved in the design and conduct of the survey.

Group-administered questionnaire. This is the most popular technique. It has the basic advantages of insuring a high degree of employee participation and minimizing administrative time—although there is some of this in the mail-questionnaire technique too. The group situation also gives employees the opportunity to ask questions. Its major drawback is the cost of employees' time off the job, or of pay if they are allowed overtime.

Choosing Types of Questions

Several types of questions can be used, individually or in combination, for surveys.

The first is the strict checklist approach, which consists of questions that demand either a yes or a no response.

In order to get a meaningful reading of attitudes, the survey designer must prepare questions that seem alike but in fact contain varying shades of meaning. This not only enables him to identify attitudes in some depth, but also helps in determining whether employees are being consistently truthful in their replies.

The second approach consists of questions that have a graduated choice of responses over a continuum. For example, the respondent can indicate reactions ranging from highly favorable to highly unfavorable. These questions can generally be completed more readily by employees than the yes-or-no type.

A third form of questions, the open-ended type, is used mainly to elicit general comments at the conclusion of a survey. Because these questions require more time to study, classify, and interpret, they are rarely employed for an entire survey, although one or two are frequently included in a closed-ended survey.

Following the design of each question, top management should consider what might be done in the event of both favorable and unfavorable responses.

Mechanics of the Project

Any survey project requires a number of basic steps. Although some of the following may seem elementary or obvious, all must be checked off regardless of the number of employees to be surveyed or the time period involved.

1. Determine the number of employees to be surveyed. If the survey is to be handled in group sessions, decide on the size of each group, timing, rate per day, and time allotted for traveling to and from the survey location.
2. Check meeting or mailing schedule with top execu-

tives to avoid conflict with other programs, and obtain approval.
3. Compile questions, pretest them, and then amend them as necessary.
4. Design final questionnaire and print it.
5. Issue advance notice to all involved.
6. Administer the survey individually, in meetings, or by mail.
7. Process the responses.
8. Analyze the responses.
9. Conduct follow-up interviews if required for clarification of opinion trends and report the results to management, including recommendations for action.
10. Report the results to employees, with stress on action decisions.

Budget has not been included in this list, although it logically fits after the first item given above. If the survey is to be conducted on company time, the value of employees' hours should be considered. The time needed for printing, interviewing, and administering the survey, and for processing, analyzing, and reporting the responses, should also be taken into account.

Advance Notice

Advance information about a survey can make the difference between good and poor response from supervisors and employees alike. Whether announced, however, by memo, at meetings, or on bulletin boards, notice of the survey need not be made more than five or ten days in advance.

Whether he first hears about a survey at the time he's asked to participate in it, or whether he first hears about it via the grapevine, the employee will wonder what the "angle" is. If the angle is demonstrated to be in his best interests, he will respond enthusiastically.

It is equally important that management and supervision be fully apprised of the purposes of the survey. This will help them overcome their apprehension, and their support and encouragement can insure greater cooperation by all employees.

The value of developing support from union leaders and stewards should not be overlooked. They should be informed about the survey after management and supervision have been, and either before or at the same time employees are told.

The next question is: Who should conduct the audit? Many companies prefer to design and conduct their own surveys, while many others call in outside personnel at some stage of the process—either when planning the survey, designing questions, conducting the survey, or analyzing responses. Using outsiders tends to assure employees of impartial and objective evaluation of results. Furthermore, outside personnel are less likely to rationalize away findings and more likely to encourage or conduct deeper investigation of disturbing trends.

Some companies also use employee committees to analyze responses and suggest corrective action.

Surveying: A Scientific Approach

Surveying is a scientific business activity, an important management tool. Like other business tools, such as data processing equipment and quality control devices, surveys must be used properly. You have to know how to:

- Write procedures and design forms properly.

- Use the right techniques, such as questionnaires or personal interviews, or both.
- Determine whether all employees or a random sampling should be used.
- Tabulate results from raw data.
- Interpret the results and recommend management action.
- Summarize the results for the participants.

Above all, you must be objective, shielding the facts from no one in top management.

Interpretive capabilities must also be considered. Facts in themselves, whether related to benefits, compensation, or any other personnel matters, can lead to false conclusions. Therefore, the analysis and recommendations should be made or at least examined by professionals with extensive experience in their specialties. The investment can pay off richly.

Taking Action

Once it is obvious that action is necessary, management should be quick to act on those matters that can be resolved easily and inexpensively. Comment should be made on any problems that are more involved or not likely to be changed. An early response by management to the results of surveys avoids the sort of employee reaction that is summarized as, "Management now knows the problem and still won't do anything about it."

One of the most serious barriers to upward communication by employees is management's failure to act on information they have received through surveys. Lack of management action is enough to cool employees entirely to any declared proclamations of sincerity. It may turn them off completely from making any further efforts to communicate.

Far more satisfying for both management and employees is the feeling, after the periodic attitude audit, that "The boss's door is always open; I can stop in any time."

Consider, for example, the case history of a company that wanted to determine ways and means of improving communications about benefits so that it could realize a better return for the money spent on employee benefits. To accomplish this goal, the company asked all exempt and nonexempt salaried personnel to complete a questionnaire designed to indicate what they thought and knew about their benefits. The responses were tabulated and analyzed, and then the completed questionnaires were destroyed so that no one in the company saw any of the responses.

In the meantime, consultants conducted depth interviews with salaried employees at representative locations. These interviews were an important and integral part of the study and they complemented the questionnaire responses. Specifically, the interviews were undertaken to:

- Corroborate the questionnaire findings.
- Identify underlying factors to responses.
- Determine the relevance and importance of write-in responses to the questionnaires.

While visiting the company's various locations, the consultants also discussed local benefits practices with management and generally looked for ways to improve these practices.

The results were then reported to management, together with recommendations for a planned benefits communication program based on the needs and opportunities revealed in the survey.

Here is an outline of the general findings:

- Most employees thought that the company was a good place to work, although some indicated that opportunities for advancement were insufficient.
- The benefits program was generally considered to be good. Vacation policy was one area employees felt to be deficient.
- Basic and major medical insurance was considered the most important benefit. Additional life insurance and life insurance after retirement were least important.
- Employees were not very knowledgeable about the specific provisions of the benefits. This was expected. The key question was: Did they want to know more? It seemed that they did, judging from the write-in questions received. Responses to another question about the extent of medical coverage also indicated they wanted to know more, but there was no consensus about the best medium for communication.
- Employees expressed desire for (1) an improvement in basic medical coverage, (2) a provision for withdrawals from stock bonus trust, and (3) an increase in early retirement benefits.

The consultants' conclusions and recommendations were carried out in detail, and additional survey work was planned.

6

Communicating Overseas

IF IT is difficult to achieve completely successful communications in North America despite the uniformity of language and education, and the relative homogeneity of culture and ideology, the communication problems overseas of a multicountry corporation are compounded in comparison.

One of the earliest realizations of a North American compensation and benefits administrator, facing a prospective European or Latin American workforce for the first time, is that despite their proximity, people in adjacent countries abroad rarely have similar histories, social structures, languages, types of government, cultures, tax or legal systems. Nor do they share the same attitudes or expectations. He is continually reminded how through history each country has developed its own national characteristics, with its people talking, acting, and thinking about things in particular ways that differentiate them from what may appear to be geographically close neighbors. Within any one nation, it is also likely that strict class structures exist and that interaction among them, except when necessary, is frowned on. Also, he becomes aware that internal splits resulting from social, political, cultural, and linguistic conflicts often exist, and further complicate national differences. At first all these factors can present an extremely difficult climate in which to communicate, and it often remains so until local skills are obtained or developed.

Language

Perhaps the most obvious problem is language—the basis of communication. Not only do languages differ from one European or Latin American nation to another; they also vary widely within certain countries. In the geographically tiny country of Belgium, the Flemish, French, and German languages are spoken in different regions. Brazil, where both Portuguese and Spanish are spoken, exemplifies the same problem in Latin America.

Within any one country, dialects may also present communication problems, even for natives. In Latin America alone, there are some twenty-five Spanish dialects, while north Germans sometimes have trouble understanding their Bavarian counterparts.

Even if an American benefits administrator can communicate in another language, he may still have serious difficulties with colloquialisms and the different connotations that are placed on certain words. In Australia, as in many Latin American and European nations, the most carefully worded communication about benefits may be doomed to failure if the word "compensation" is used to mean salary and benefits. True, the word signifies that to Canadian and American employees, but in other areas of the world it often implies something akin to workmen's compensation for an accident or illness and has nothing to do with salary or other types of benefits. Outside North America, the word "remuneration" conveys the American concept of compensation.

"Profits" is another word often found in American communications about benefits which should be used with care elsewhere. Although the word exists in almost every language, it may be considered a pejorative word connoting exploitation in almost any other part of the world. If a profit-sharing plan is to be instituted overseas, the United States company must first recognize the need for educating the employee group on the positive aspects and desirability of profits. Only after such preliminaries have cleared the way can and should the plan be communicated.

The frequently used phrase "coverage for you [the employee] and your family" has led to unexpected problems for some American and European companies with operations in African countries. The problem was caused by both language and cultural differences of which the newcomers were not aware. The African concept of an employee's family could include several wives (each with children), in-laws, brothers, sisters, parents, grandparents, other relatives, and even friends. If a more careful study of the culture had been made, the company could have avoided the unfortunate phraseology.

In Latin America, the meaning of many basic management communications—and these frequently deal with benefits—are often clouded by the American company's use of the word "corporation." To the North American, this word means a large industrial organization. To the Latin American, it connotes a financial institution such as a bank.

There are also a multitude of words which simply defy precise translation. For example, "management incentive plan" may translate into something suggesting a "piecerate program," which is much below the dignity of the managers to whom it would be applied.

Most of these problems could be avoided if companies with overseas offices emphasized the importance of both a knowledge of and a sensitivity toward the language in which they must communicate.

One way to alleviate some of these problems is to give local nationals an important voice in helping communicate data about benefits and other management policies. Such people possess the knowledge and necessary language sensitivity, even though they may need training in communication techniques. However, the latter skill is usually much easier to master than the former.

Culture

Although language presents obvious difficulties when communicating abroad, variations in the cultural makeup of different nations can pose just as many problems. Each country has its own unique likes and dislikes, social musts and taboos, prides and prejudices, and habits of housing, dress, and eating. Business varies, too, with respect to corporate structure and outlook; degree of government involvement; social responsibility; management education, selection, and training; attitudes toward executive mobility, organized labor, motivation, and compensation; types and levels of benefits; and, of course, communications.

All these and more deep-rooted variations exist, covering every facet of public, business, and private life. For instance, a small businessman in France will rarely be persuaded to take a business risk, widen his distribution area, or raise a bank loan for long-term expansion. He's been trained, and legislation still encourages him to think first of security, to play safe. The honor, success, and standing of his company means the honor, success, and standing of his family. It is traditional for larger French companies to hire graduates from the five great engineering schools for top management positions. Marked as cadres, or management elite, from the minute they are hired, they are the only personnel who can make it to the top.

In Belgium, the land of the giant holding companies, university engineers have a much greater chance of becoming cadres, and it helps if they have chosen their parents carefully. Engineers who have been educated in a technical college rather than a university are paid less, and expect less, throughout their career than do university-educated engineers doing exactly the same work. Although such class consciousness has lessened in recent years, companies which buck the system must still do so with caution. Technical engineers may have less access to government circles and to trade and management associations. There is also the chance that a management team may walk out if a nonuniversity-educated engineer is installed in a superior position to them.

In Italy, executives called *dirigenti* have a union of their own to bargain for them on salary and benefits matters. Middle management is often not given enough information or authority to do its job effectively. This situation exists partly because of top management's tendency toward authoritarianism and partly because of a fear of information leakage to the tax inspector. In a land where tax evasion is a national pastime, business efficiency suffers.

In Germany, the employers' associations are dominated by *Unternehmer*, that is, entrepreneurs with small firms, and not by professional managers of large companies. The nonowner/manager may be envied by his business associates for his status and income, but he is also regarded as inferior to the *Unternehmer* because he is risking someone else's money. The idea of control divorced from ownership is gaining acceptance very slowly in Germany.

The only European workers who have much chance of making it to the top are the English and the Germans. In Belgium, France, and Italy, the highest level a worker is likely to reach is foreman; and in France he's not even regarded as a member of the management team. There are exceptions, of course; but they're rare.

This background sets the stage for the differences in the attitudes of government, employer, and worker toward benefits.

In Germany there exists a carry-over from medieval feudalism called the *Fürsorgepflicht* concept; that is, the German manager mirrors the feudal lord's duty to care for his vassals. Many German pension plans are funded through book reserves, and in the event of bankruptcy, the worker and the retiree have little assurance of getting their benefits. And yet, because workers have seen bank savings and investments disappear again and again during inflation and because they believe that companies emerge intact after inflation, they are content to trust in the *Fürsorgepflicht* of their companies.

In Italy, as in Germany, management tends to be paternalistic and very concerned for the workers' welfare. Many large companies provide housing, medical facilities, and even day-care nurseries, together with a host of other fringes.

Most benefits in Italy are provided by the state. Management contributes a very high percentage of payroll to support the Social Security program. Private plans are not common and aren't usually expected. Those that do exist usually provide token benefits to show the employer's interest in his people and to reward long service.

Business practices in Italy can be better understood by examining the history, structure, and objectives of organized labor. Because of the widespread unemployment before World War II, people had an overriding concern for security. During Italy's postwar industrialization, labor relations were dominated by crippling strikes and strong, politically oriented unions which battled with government and management to increase workers' security. Although strikes still occur, the unions are not only experiencing diminishing support but are also beginning to realize that they are pointing in the wrong direction. Workers are more secure and are beginning to see the sense of working *with* management to achieve mutual goals.

In France, class barriers are quite strong, and different groups often act like separate societies who accidentally happen to share the same geographic region. French unions are politically motivated and are structured to exert immense pressure at the national level. However, they are less strong regionally and usually lack the organization to exert effective pressure at the shop-floor level, as they can in Great Britain.

In terms of benefits, there is also evidence of French class consciousness at work, to the point where a separate nationwide fund is set up to cover the management elite—the cadres. The pensions accruing from these funds are much higher as a percentage of pay than are those paid to other employees, who are covered by another fund.

In Switzerland another set of attitudes and expectations prevail. Employees, management, and government all generally accept the thesis that it's the individual's responsibility to safeguard his own future. The Swiss have traditionally been known as more frugal and savings-conscious than other peoples. They live less flamboyantly in general and have less regard for material possessions as status symbols than people in other countries. Moreover, the Swiss government pays a uniform pension amount below subsistence level, as it were, to start each employee's savings. Employers feel that they too should show an interest and do so by adding another portion to their employees' retirement income.

The individual does the rest. The independent nature of the Swiss employee is further seen in the fact that he usually has his own private medical insurance. Also, his contributions to Social Security are based on *total* income, although he knows that his pension may be based on only part of his income.

In Holland too, Social Security provides benefits below a subsistence level. It's interesting to note, however, that 80 percent of covered earnings, which is a very high rate, is paid as a disability pension. This suggests that the Dutch think that the rules of the save-it-yourself game are broken when a man is disabled. But this save-it-yourself concept is illustrated even more clearly by the fact that only the employee contributes toward Social Security old age and survivors' pensions.

These thumbnail sketches show the different backgrounds and cultures in relation to the different behavior patterns, concepts, attitudes, and expectations they foster. And since there is an almost universal suspicion toward the "outsider"—especially toward the American investor, who is often the object of a love-hate syndrome—it is imperative that American companies not unintentionally offend through faulty communications of any management policy, including benefits. Poor impressions caused by getting off on the wrong foot make bridging the cultural gap an uphill climb. The more successful firms are those which promote a good image by immediately establishing and maintaining public or community relations programs geared to presenting themselves as responsible corporate citizens.

Such a program should:

1. Explain company objectives, allaying fears of exploitation.
2. Reflect the company's permanence in the new location, alluding to the benefit programs and their long-range growth.
3. Rely on local personnel for cultural know-how; that is, what's expected and accepted in the area.
4. Keep an ear to the local grapevine so that any rumors can be put to rest before they cause undue damage.

However, a good corporate image cannot carry over into communications about benefits if the American management bypasses the local culture and adheres to the philosophy that the American way is the best way and the only way. Just as benefits planners are aware that a worker in Buffalo doesn't expect, or necessarily need, the same benefits as a worker in Milan, so the successful benefits communicator must follow the same cultural principles.

American industries are often accused by those outside the United States of being wholly devoted to the precept that money is the most important motivator. Perhaps people in other nations agree that money is important. However, for a variety of reasons, including high tax rates on direct remuneration (salary and bonuses), few employers promote the concept as do Americans. Therefore, when planning and communicating information about benefits to non-Americans, United States companies should put direct remuneration into the perspective of the employees of each particular locale. Often a message about benefits which emphasizes a shorter work week or a longer vacation period will have much more impact than a message which deals with an increase in salary.

A sensitivity to culture, as to language, must be acquired in order to tell the story about benefits. And, as in the case of language, more than one culture may prevail in one country. The requirement for communicating in French in the province of Quebec provides an excellent example.

It is said that communications makes up 90 percent of the management process in the United States. This is also true in North America, with communications often accountable for profit or loss, success or failure. Poor communications from an outside organization can unintentionally affront local traditions or life styles and, consequently, estrange not only employees but the community as a whole. It's also easy for an outsider to miss subtle changes in the local social and business climate. To avoid such problems or to rectify them quickly if they occur, active listening posts and reliable feedback systems must also be a part of any program of communications about benefits.

Other Employee Audiences

In addition to the local national, two other employee audiences usually receive information about benefits from the foreign-based American company. One audience consists of United States expatriates—American citizens working in a foreign location. The other consists of third-country nationals (TCNs), employees of the corporation who are neither Americans nor citizens of the country in which they are working. These people often make a career out of being international employees and might be considered members of the international cadre. Because of the highly individualistic and complex benefits programs needed to adequately compensate these two employee groups, communications to them pose unique problems.

The U.S. expatriate is usually an exceptional employee who has been given a difficult task. In most instances, he and his family have been moved lock, stock, and barrel to a strange environment. He holds an important position in a foreign country where he must function effectively despite problems caused by language and cultural differences. In essence, his family's entire life style is threatened with change.

Most U.S. multinational companies agree that the role of expatriate employees is not an easy one. Because of this, it is common practice to compensate them handsomely. Aside from having regular salary and bonus arrangements, they are ordinarily awarded allowances or premiums for reparation for the cultural shock encountered by living outside North America; travel costs for home leaves; cost-of-living expenses, such as housing, tax equalization, or education for their children; and increased entertainment costs.

All told, the expatriate ends up earning substantially more than his counterparts with similar or even greater responsibilities who are local nationals or TCNs. Their situation calls for highly professional, sensitive, and sophisticated international techniques for communicating information about benefits.

Where there is a lack of definitive communications, expatriates often account for their financial status by adopting the attitude that they are somehow worth more than other employees and are, therefore, entitled to receive more from the corporation. Expatriates must be impressed with the actual reasons why they are receiving greater compensation so that they do not cause animosity by promoting the image of their own superiority.

The same story must be told to local nationals and TCNs, since they will probably be aware of the expatriate's greater compensation and resent it. Without adequate communications concerning the rationale of expatriate compensation, the others may quickly conclude that the U.S. company is favoring its own, or worse, exploiting non-American personnel.

The need for this type of communication becomes evident when you realize that in many U.S. companies relatively low-level expatriate executives earn more than the foreign-born managing director.

The TCN's compensation problems surpass those of the local national and the expatriate. Moreover, the increased mobility of young executives, especially in Europe, has caused the number of TCNs working for U.S. firms overseas to grow.

When a TCN transfers from one country to another, his base salary in the country from which he is coming (not necessarily his home country) may be higher or lower than that for a comparable position in a new country. Cost of living, taxes, inflation, local laws, and established practices within the country of assignment must also be considered.

Long-range financial security, like pensions and Social Security, present difficulties for this group in areas such as funding, collecting, taxation, and currency restrictions. Pensions, for example, are usually set up in the TCN's home country, if the U.S. employer has operations there. If this is not the case, perhaps an offshore fund will be used, such as those that have been established in the Bahamas, Bermuda, Liechtenstein, or Curacao. Social Security payments are also an issue, since they can often be totally or partially lost to the TCN if he does not meet certain residency requirements.

Because of the confusing nature of TCN benefits, communications must be lucid and must stress the financial security so important to the TCN. Communications to this group about benefits should also emphasize the flexibility of the company's approach to TCN compensation and should explain in detail all methods of producing fair and equitable benefits, such as offshore funds. Also, the TCN's compensation must be placed in the perspective of the U.S. expatriate's and local national's compensation to avoid misunderstandings.

Finally, the TCN, like the local national, is not an American, so he presents language and cultural problems to the benefits communicator. These problems are often multiple, since the TCN employee group in any U.S. firm in any location may represent many languages and cultures.

In Conclusion

Because of the degree of sophistication required and the large stakes involved, international programs of communications about benefits should be handled only by the seasoned professional. Even he can make an unintentional but embarrassing or costly error simply because so many crucial factors affect every communication.

The basic tenets of effective benefits communications abroad are as follows:

1. Research concerning the language and the culture of the foreign location, as well as that of the various countries represented by the TCNs, must be conducted and understood.

2. A sensitivity to these languages and cultures must be developed, preferably with the assistance of nationals.
3. The specific problems of various employee groups (culture, language, benefits, and so forth) must be assessed.
4. Communications must be developed which keep the preceding factors in mind.
5. Feedback channels must be kept open in order to constantly review results, stop rumors, and correct misunderstandings or unintentional errors.

International communications about benefits, however, cannot and should not stand alone. They must be accompanied by a total communications effort of management policies and procedures. The effectiveness of the one is truly dependent on the other. Working together, they pave the way for the U.S. company's successful operations abroad.

7

Communicating About Direct Compensation

Not long ago, a national magazine carried a cartoon of a conversation between a new employee and the company's personnel manager. After telling the employee what his salary would be, the personnel manager said, "Please do not divulge your salary to any of your fellow workers." The employee replied, "You have nothing to worry about. I'm just as embarrassed about it as you are."

Joking aside, secrecy about salaries is hardly unusual. Many companies willingly discuss products, customer relations, manufacturing problems, profits and losses, and other facets of the business with employees, and most are thoroughly convinced of the importance of communicating benefits information. But when it comes to pay, no violet could be more shrinking.

Why do companies have pay policies, spend vast amounts of money on salary administration programs, or go to great lengths to develop intricate compensation plans? Obviously, they do so to attract and then to keep the caliber of people who make that organization successful. A typical salary administration plan provides for pay that is equitable within the organization and competitive with that provided by other employers in the industry and in the community.

Such plans, however, are also designed to recognize, motivate, and reward employees. Unless he sees direct evidence, how can an employee believe that his talents have been recognized? How can he be motivated to do a better job or convinced that his efforts are being adequately rewarded? If he does not know the parameters of other jobs within his company and what those jobs pay, why should he aspire to greater heights or attempt to develop his own potential? It seems just common sense to tell employees as much as possible about a subject so near and dear to their hearts.

Unfortunately, communicating pay information is not that simple. Many considerations must be taken into account that do not exist, for example, when communicating about benefits. Benefits are frequently the same for everyone, or a uniform formula applies across the board, or the supplier of services is a third party over whom no one has direct control. When communicating pay information, however, you are dealing with a very personal subject and more directly with personalities. Moreover, the preparation of salary programs is far from an exact science. No matter how carefully they are designed to be equitable, subjective elements are bound to exist. And the administration of such a program is also subjective in nature. How, then, do you determine what to communicate?

How Much to Communicate

The president of one company was frequently pestered, directly or through innuendo, by his vice-presidents and other top managerial people to give his views on how they stacked up against each other. One morning he posted a notice on the bulletin board near his office. It read: "You often ask me how I feel about you. Here's my answer." There followed a list of names, the salary each was getting, and each one's bonus for the year.

In another company, an employee was surprised and a little confused one day to find his pay check larger than usual. Was it a mistake? Very likely, he thought, because no one had told him he was getting a raise. In fact, no one had ever discussed performance or pay with him, or, for that matter, with any one else in the company. When he finally asked his supervisor about the check, he learned, happily, that he had indeed received a raise.

These situations represent two extremes on the communications scale—telling all or telling nothing.

Telling All

Is it wise to tell all your employees everything about your job structure, the various grades in it, and the ranges for each? Even, perhaps, who is in each grade? Suppose you believe you have a very good salary administration program. You're proud of it—it's fair and equitable—and you believe it would be to your advantage to tell your employees what a good thing they have.

Professor Edward E. Lawler of Yale University would advise you to do so. In a study of 500 managers representing a variety of companies, he found that people tend to overestimate the pay levels of their peers and subordinates while underestimating the earnings of their supervisors.[1] He believes that this tendency leads to a lowering of morale and motivation.

On the other hand, government agencies at every level publish all such information about their jobs. Civil service, of course, is not private industry. Government jobs are tax supported and public communication becomes a necessity for political reasons.

Some companies operate on a "star" system to encourage competition among employees. Because salaries and bonuses are published, the star enjoys the limelight, and the losers presumably grit their teeth and prepare to work harder during the next round.

There are, however, some very real dangers in such widespread, no-secrets-barred communications. First, no matter how good a program a company may have, telling the whole story leaves it open to employees' judgments and criticisms. As mentioned earlier, many of the decisions in developing the program are necessarily subjective and could be questioned by anyone with differing opinions. Secondly, most employees simply do not have the background to understand the implications and ramifications of a salary administration program. Thirdly, this question must be asked: Does a company have the *right* to let each employee know how much every other employee earns? Most companies believe a man's earnings, like his private life, are strictly his own business. If he wants to trade information with others, that is up to him.

Keeping Quiet

There's an axiom in the communications business to the

[1] "The Mythology of Management Compensation," *California Management Review*, vol. 9, no. 1, Fall 1966.

effect that no communication is some communication. And human nature being what it is, the employee who gets little or no information about his company's salary administration program is likely to conclude that the program is deficient. Of course, in some instances this is quite true, and may be a very good reason for not communicating. But in other situations it isn't true—although many employees will still believe it is. And since pay is a form of recognition, much of the program's value is lost if people are not informed about it. They may also tend to do a less effective job if they feel that additional effort is unappreciated. Worse, they may look elsewhere for the psychic and financial recognition they want.

In one case, a company was very happy with a bright, aggressive young man and had great plans for his future. He surprised them one day by resigning to take a job elsewhere that he thought had a better future. He was equally surprised to learn that the company he was leaving had plans for him, since no one had told him how well he was doing or what his future possibilities were. In a last-ditch effort, the company offered him a higher salary than the new job would pay. But it was too late; he had already committed himself.

Between the Two Extremes

Since too much and too little communication both present hazards, the logical question is: How much is advisable?

The answer will depend on the attitudes and personality of the company, its goals, its situation in the job market, the type of business it is in, its credibility with employees, the quality of its management, its salary program, and other factors.

Some aspects of pay policies can be broadcast to all employees. Others are perhaps better confined to the management group. However, there is probably more individual, face-to-face, personal communication required in pay policies than in almost any other dealings between employer and employees.

Salary administration programs must, of course, be updated from time to time. Individual jobs become more complex, new jobs are added, and some old positions change in character. Or a company that never had a formal program may decide to put one into operation.

At such times, the wise company communicates to everyone by announcing the fact that a study is under way, the reasons for it, what it is expected to accomplish, and the value of the new or improved program to employees. The company may spell out specifics, such as who will be conducting the study, those employees whose cooperation will be needed, and the length of time the study is expected to take. In this way management can allay any fears about salary cuts and at the same time dampen any expectations of overly large increases in salaries.

There are a number of ways to communicate this kind of information. A series of articles in the company magazine or newspaper may be sufficient. A slide or chart presentation to groups of employees may be preferred since it permits two-way discussion and an immediate forum for questions. If outside experts are involved in the study, their presence at the meetings may help give credence and stature to the program. Also, a printed folder highlighting various aspects of the study may be distributed at the meetings or even stand on its own.

Once a salary administration program has been established and is operating, employees should be reminded periodically of its existence and its objectives. The company magazine generally provides a good medium for this information.

Many companies distribute handbooks to employees in which some mention is made of pay policies. All too frequently, however, these communications are confined to bland or obvious statements such as "Merit increases are granted periodically." Here, too, a company with a good salary administration program can spell out the broader objectives and mechanics of the program in more explicit terms to assure employees that they are, indeed, being paid fairly and equitably.

The Company and Competition

One of the most important measurements used in designing and revising salary administration programs is the relationship of compensation within the company to what the competition is paying, within both the industry and the community.

This is another area in which companies can communicate effectively. The company may need to sell the value of its program to management, because it is the attitudes of management—especially at middle and lower levels—that help formulate attitudes among the rank and file.

Some progressive companies hold meetings on a regular basis, such as once or twice a year, to inform managers where the company stands in the compensation competition. At times, this type of information is discussed with special groups of employees, such as scientists or engineers, who hold "professional" attitudes that differ from those held by other employees. There is also a variety of subcultures today in companies whose members are linked more by common personal interests than by company loyalties. Divorced men and ethnic groups are examples.

For different reasons, these people need to know that their company's compensation is competitive, and that financially, at least, job changing will not solve their other problems.

Who Needs to Know?

What about the specifics of a salary program, that is, the actual salary ranges for each job, where each employee in the job stands, what the year's bonuses were, and similar information? How much and how far should this information be communicated?

Since every salary program requires that one or more persons appraise others in one way or another, and that recommendations be made about salary increases or promotions, certain people of necessity require this information. For example, managers know the salaries of their staff members, and supervisors know the salaries of their subordinates.

Then there is the individual, at any level. Obviously each employee needs to be told what he will earn for the year and the bonus, if any, he is to receive. Do you tell him anything beyond that? How wise is it to discuss his salary range, where he stands in it, how far he has yet to go before reaching the maximum? Some companies believe an employee should have at least this much information; others believe it is telling too much. Here are some expressions of opinion by experts in the field on both sides of this question. First, those in favor:

- "Pay is a form of recognition, which means that some people get more than others. Unless this fact is communicated, no one knows he's been recognized."
- "Most people like to know how high is high."

- "If someone is close to the maximum, he should know that his increases are limited. Otherwise his expectations are too high."
- "Each employee should know his own range and the range of the next grade so that he can tell how high he can go."
- "If a company has a good salary program, it has a justifiable answer to any questions an employee might raise."
- "Questions from employees that cannot be satisfactorily answered may reveal weaknesses in the salary structure, which means it needs adjustment or revision."
- "If you do not communicate, you are dodging your responsibility to your employees."
- "You can assume that your employees are aware of what the competition pays and that they will judge your program on that basis. You might as well let people know."
- "People should know when the next salary review is scheduled—whether it is in six months, one year, or two years—so they can relax and get on with the job in the meantime. Otherwise they become uneasy."

Those opposed to giving employees more than a certain amount of information about their benefits cite these reasons:

- "If an employee is happy with the pay increase he received, you could make him unhappy by telling him the 'average' increase that year was higher."
- "You eliminate the element of pleasant surprise at a raise when the employee knows the limits of his pay range."
- "By telling an employee the salary range for his job,

you box him in, leaving him with a sense of frustration or futility since he cannot go beyond—except possibly by promotion or an adjustment in the program."
- "Performance appraisals and handing out pay raises should be separated, because the latter may have no connection to the former. However, the employee is likely to think they are related and be unhappy if he does not think the raise is enough."
- "Telling an employee too much raises his expectations too high."
- "All an employee needs to have is a feeling of trust that someone in the company will assess his performance and not ignore him, that his pay level will be competitive, that the cost of living will be taken into account, that there is some internal equity, and that his pay will actually be reviewed. He does not need to know the specifics to keep his morale high."
- "Employees do not have to be satisfied with their pay. Lack of satisfaction can motivate."

Conclusion

Communicating information about pay is not only important but vitally necessary. Our society is deeply committed to the importance of achievement as a measure of worth. And although a man's sphere of achievement will vary depending on his background, education, experience, and other factors, people in business do measure their achievements. In a work situation, the most obvious measure of that achievement is pay.

Although some will argue to the contrary, it does seem true that a full-blown effort to communicate salary information is probably not the best way to motivate employees. There are too many variables in establishing salary grades in different areas of a company's business for the total working population in that organization to understand. And people are primarily interested in their own jobs; their interest in other jobs is usually limited to comparisons and is usually active only when that comparison makes them look good.

Although broad concepts can be broadly communicated, the most effective communication is likely to take place in a face-to-face situation. And in this area there is much room for improvement. A major reason for the ineffectivenes of face-to-face communication and for avoiding responsibility for that communication is the lack of knowledge on the part of managers and supervisors of *how* to communicate with employees.

Considering all the money companies spend developing salary administration programs and other financial incentives, it would seem sensible to spend a little more money educating management personnel to communicate more effectively about them. It is possible to learn to recognize different types of personalities among company employees. It is also possible to learn to talk to people in their frame of reference instead of your own, and to develop a favorable instead of an unfavorable interchange. The value of such education offers far greater advantages than a periodic review of pay or performance. Such education can result in better employee relations the year round, in the achievement of corporate and individual goals, and in the development of a more dynamic organization.

8

Six Case Studies

American Airlines

American Airlines, which has main offices in New York and hundreds of branch offices in the United States and abroad, believes in benefits communications. As William Fisher, supervisor of benefits planning, puts it, "The company realizes that it is of little value to have a solid program of benefits if we can't tell our employees about them in a clear, understandable manner."

The company employs some 36,000 persons, 1,000 of whom came to American as a result of a 1971 merger with Trans-Caribbean Airways. These fairly new employees, many of whom are more familiar with Spanish than English, have been introduced to the variety of benefits available to them from American Airlines through a booklet (available in either language) which is used as a basis for discussion in meetings with first-line supervisors.

American Airlines has an especially well-rounded benefits program, with appeal to both older and younger employees. A distinctive feature is discount vacation travel for employees and their families on the company's planes. In addition, vacationing employees receive discounts on hotels, car rentals, tours, and so on. These benefits attract new employees and retain them. Older employees, to whom jet setting has less appeal, are more gratified by the company's pension and insurance plans.

First-line supervisors are the key to effective benefits communications at American. "Get the information to the first-line supervisor," Mr. Fisher says, "and he'll sell it to the employees." To determine their effectiveness as communicators, the airline intends to survey a representative sampling of first-line supervisors to discover how much they really know about the company's benefits, the calculation of pensions, and so on. The ultimate objective of this study is to develop training modules in areas where the supervisors lack sufficient knowledge.

The actual planning of benefits communications originates with Mr. Fisher. The company's Insurance Administration Department compiles the booklets which form the cornerstone of the communications program. An employee newspaper, *Astrojet News*, gives general information about changes in benefits.

In addition, each year employees receive a brief computerized statement of their retirement benefits. The company plans to expand the scope of this statement in the future to make it the most effective means of communicating benefits to its employees.

Employee attitude surveys are administered by the company whenever the need arises. They are designed and interpreted by internal specialists. A recent survey was conducted to determine what cargo handlers thought of their compensation and benefits. Although the employees' general attitude was favorable, the study revealed that benefits meant less both pragmatically and psychologically to employees working in major metropolitan areas than they did to employees working in less urban locales.

American Airlines takes pride in its program of pre-retirement counseling. Five years prior to retirement, employees meet in small groups with a trained counselor and view a slide presentation covering all aspects of the subject. During the next few years, supervisors counsel any interested employee on an individual basis. A year before the scheduled retirement date, small group-discussion meetings begin, supplemented by published materials. The primary aim is to prepare the employee emotionally for life as a retiree—but practical aspects of retirement, including benefits provided by the company, are also stressed. Because American Airlines believes its benefits programs are among the best in the industry, it is making as great an effort as possible to insure that employees believe it too.

Columbia Gas System

Columbia Gas offers its 12,000 employees five major benefit plans, encompassing provisions for retirement, disability, thrift, health, and life insurance. Since the organization is spread across much of the eastern United States in a variety of locations, it maintains five group headquarters—in Pittsburgh, Houston, Columbus, Charleston (West Virginia), and Ashland (Kentucky). At corporate headquarters in Wilmington, Delaware, the manager of internal communications, Bennett Smith, assists the employee benefits department in planning programs for benefits communications.

Mr. Smith describes the aim of benefits communications

programs at Columbia Gas as being "not so much to explain the intricate details of benefits to the employees—we can never hope to make them experts—but to leave them with the firm knowledge that they enjoy excellent benefits about which detailed information is always available."

That "detailed information" is disseminated in a variety of forms. In 1970, after three benefit plans were changed significantly, the company embarked on a five-step communications program.

The first step was the mailing of an announcement brochure to all employees that explained the changes in general terms.

The announcement was followed by the showing of a videotape to all employees. The tape featured a benefits expert who used slides and chalk board to illustrate the intricate details of the changes. The meetings, which were conducted by personnel from the employee relations departments in the groups, were held at some 300 Columbia locations, and included a question-answer period.

Step three was the preparation of feature articles for employee magazines that are published at group levels. The articles provide background information on the changes.

Until recently, benefits booklets were mailed to employees' homes. This practice is in the process of being phased out in favor of a looseleaf binder (step four) that will provide a complete one-step reference guide.

Step five is a series of black-and-white posters featuring photographs of individual employees. Beneath each picture is the employee's own statement of how a certain Columbia benefit helped him. Seven of these testimonial posters were prepared for bulletin boards at Columbia's work locations.

Control Data Corporation

Founded in 1957, this company is primarily engaged in the development, design, manufacture, and marketing of a broad line of computer systems and associated peripheral devices. It employs approximately 28,000 persons in the United States on a full-time basis.

Discussing the company's communications philosophy, Byron Johnson, corporate director of compensation, says, "We believe that an informed employee is a better employee." This attitude is attested to by the attention given to communications about benefits. Planning for this activity is done every six months. Projects are usually handled by Mr. Johnson and his staff, with the editorial assistance of the Employee Communication Department.

Recent projects include:

- Production of a half-hour, open-circuit television program (yet to be telecast) designed to demonstrate how the family of a Control Data employee is affected by his benefits.
- Development of a claims kit which includes all forms needed to file any kind of a claim, plus instructions needed to fill them out properly.
- Production of a videotape program to explain to employees how the company's salary administration program operates.

Individual benefit plans are outlined in a looseleaf binder which all employees receive. The plans are covered in more detail in individual booklets. The company also uses payroll inserts, hospital admission cards, and an employees' annual report to educate and remind employees about their benefits. On one occasion, the company also issued a personalized, computer-produced benefits statement. Because of the costs involved, however, future statements will be issued less frequently than once a year.

Upward communications receive no less attention. Formal attitude surveys are conducted on a corporatewide basis with smaller preselected groups, at irregular intervals and have led to changes in benefits and compensation practices. Monthly meetings conducted by the general managers of the divisions are also a good source of feedback. All employees reporting to the manager attend, and he is required to submit a report to the president of the company detailing their reactions to subjects discussed and listing the questions they asked. The latter are frequently answered by the president in a newsletter he issues. Employee question boxes, a formal grievance procedure, and exit interviews also provide valuable input to help guide further downward communication efforts.

Mr. Johnson foresees the day when Control Data Corporation will provide employees with a basic core of benefits and a wide choice of options. And this approach, he feels, will require better communications than ever before.

Hallmark Cards Incorporated

America's leading producer of greeting cards and other social-expression products employs some 8,500 persons on a full-time basis in the United States. The great majority are located at corporate headquarters in Kansas City, Missouri, and in plants in neighboring Kansas.

The company's Career Rewards Program is composed of an unusually broad variety of benefits. Its major components are retirement, profit-sharing, thrift, life insurance, medical insurance, and long- and short-term disability plans; business travel and voluntary accident insurance plans; and an educational assistance program. Also included are substantial discounts on Hallmark products and other merchandise sold through a company-owned department store. Frank McClure, the man in charge of compensation and benefits at Hallmark, says, "We try to impress employees with the scope of the program rather than with the excellence of any one plan. This means there is a lot to tell employees about."

Hallmark uses a variety of media to explain its program. The basic reference piece is a series of ten booklets, attractively packaged in a vinyl, three-pocket packet. Eight of the booklets describe individual benefit plans; the other two deal with personnel policies and estate planning matters. Personal statements are issued quarterly for the profit-sharing and thrift plans and annually for the program as a whole. Several employee-oriented publications, including *Noon News*, a daily newspaper, frequently carry news and feature stories about benefits.

Face-to-face communications are also stressed. The first such exposure an employee usually has to the program occurs during the employment interview, when the long-term financial implications of the program are explained to him. The interviewer uses a special form that projects the values of the profit-sharing, thrift, and retirement plans based on the applicant's starting pay, years of service until retirement, and other factors. Upon hire, the employee receives a general explanation of his benefits at an orientation meeting. Then, as he becomes eligible for each plan in the program (over a two-year period), sessions of a more detailed nature are held.

Regular departmental meetings also provide a forum for discussions about benefits. These may be led by the department manager or by Mr. McClure or one of his associates. Finally, each employee is assigned a personnel representative who is available to counsel him on benefits matters and to assist him in filling out forms. In the past, managers also had private conferences with their subordinates to review and explain the information contained in their benefits statements. This practice was discontinued when an attitude survey showed that a substantial number of employees resented the fact that managers had access to the information in their statements. Now, group meetings are held with managers to review a John Doe statement.

To keep employee interest in the program high, Hallmark follows a policy of improving benefits frequently. As Mr. McClure puts it, "We try to make at least some improvement each year. Even if it's just a reduction in employee contributions or a relatively minor increase in benefits, it gives us something to talk about." Likewise, the company deliberately changes the format of its descriptions of benefits every three to five years in the belief that employees will reread the material if it is presented to them in a new form. Such changes are relatively easy and economical to make because of the company's internal production resources.

Upward communications receive no less attention. Periodic attitude surveys are the basic device, although the company also relies heavily on reports from personnel representatives, questions asked at meetings, letters to the editors of employee publications, and its suggestion system to determine what employees think and feel about their benefits.

Hallmark also believes it makes good sense to communicate about direct compensation. When it updated its salary administration program several years ago, virtually all employees were affected. Anticipating broad interest, Hallmark first published a series of articles in *Noon News*. These explained why a revised program was needed and how it would work, stressing that it would provide more equitable treatment for all concerned. The initial article notified employees that no one's salary would be reduced. Following the appearance of the articles, employees attended small group meetings where the revised program was explained in detail by specially trained meeting leaders using flip charts. Finally, each employee had an individual conference with his supervisor where he was informed of his salary grade, its maximum and minimum, as well as any increase in his rate.

In looking toward the future, Mr. McClure sees Hallmark's greatest challenge of benefits communications as the ability to create interest and appreciation of the program among newer and younger employees. "Longer-service people have seen the program in action over the years and they know it is among the best," he says, "so we want to concentrate on our younger people." He has, however, no major changes in mind. "We feel what we've been doing right along works very well. So we intend to keep on doing it, at least until we see a reason to change."

Reynolds Metals

This company is one of the three largest manufacturers of aluminum products in the United States. Headquartered in Richmond, Virginia, with more than 65 plant and other field locations, plus numerous sales branches, Reynolds employs some 35,000 people, about 75 percent of whom are unionized. The many benefits programs available to them are planned and administered by Richard L. Adams, manager of the Employee Security Division, with assistance from the company's Personnel and Industrial Relations Departments, as well as an outside management consultant firm and an insurance company.

The main goal of the company's communications efforts is to be sure that the average Reynolds employee understands his benefits. Another important objective is to transmit to employees the financial and emotional value of the company's contributions to their well-being. Mr. Adams believes that instilling in its employees a real appreciation of the company's active interest in them will increase morale and loyalty and also attract new, highly qualified employees. But he admits to some uncertainty about the ultimate value of benefits communications. "Frankly, it is questionable whether you ever fully develop the employee appreciation aspect, particularly among hourly workers," he says. "Unions promote the idea that the company gives the employees only those benefits which are legally settled upon in negotiations, and that without the expense of these benefits, workers' paychecks would be greater—ergo, employees are actually paying for their benefits by taking a cut in pay." Salaried workers, he comments, believe that their benefits depend upon what unions can obtain for the hourly workers, since changes and improvements in salaried benefits are engendered by union agreements. He thinks that all employees tend to take benefits for granted, as they do Social Security; thus the company gets little or no credit for its financial contribution to benefit plans.

Newly hired hourly employees receive booklets and copies of official documents which describe the benefits to which they are entitled. As changes in these benefits occur, hourly employees are first notified through announcement brochures, then through revised booklets and group meetings. Supplementing these efforts are articles in the company's monthly magazine, *The Reynolds Review.*

Salaried employees are also informed of the details of their benefits upon hire through booklets and official documents. Later they receive further information in small group meetings. The Employee Security Division trains industrial relations and personnel managers from locations outside Richmond so that they can explain changes in benefits to their salaried employees in small groups. Salaried employees also receive announcement brochures and booklets about revised benefits when changes occur. Articles in the company magazine supplement this information.

Only salaried employees receive a personal, computerized statement of the value of their own benefits each year, but hourly employees will eventually get them too. The statements are mailed to employees' homes, so that their families can also be exposed to the value of Reynolds' benefits. Salaried workers also see a slide presentation which dissects a John Doe statement, explaining in detail the meaning of each entry.

Mr. Adams believes that these personalized statements, particularly in conjunction with face-to-face discussions and the explanations provided by the slide presentation, are the most effective means of informing the employee about his benefits and encouraging his understanding and appreciation of the company's contribution to his security. The computerized statements tell employees exactly what they have; the explanatory meetings, which include plenty of time for questions, enhance their understanding.

Reynolds' current annual benefits budget is $41 million. An additional $74,000 to $85,000 is budgeted for communications about benefits. Mr. Adams believes that this is not nearly enough, and that an amount equal to at least 1 percent of the total cost of Reynolds' benefits should be appropriated for benefits communications. The use of the computerized benefit statement during the past five years has increased the benefits communications budget, but substantially more money is needed to extend this medium to hourly employees.

In 1969, Reynolds administered an attitude survey to discover in what ways employees thought the company could improve both its benefits and its communications about them. Responses led to plan revisions, such as making the major medical plan noncontributory, with a lower deductible. Other suggested changes were studied, but were not implemented because they were economically unfeasible. Studies to gauge the effectiveness of Reynolds' benefits plans and communications are conducted whenever management sees a need for them.

During strikes, the company accelerates its communications to employees' homes, pointedly describing in registered letters the value of lost wages and benefits, and setting forth clearly the offers of management to the union. The company tries to stimulate worker and family appreciation of the company's offers, not to mention a greater interest in going back to work.

Future plans include the possibility of a movie about Reynolds' benefits and more meetings of small groups of employees to discuss questions and problems concerning benefits, since face-to-face communication is considered an invaluable tool for purposes of both information and morale. Another possible project for the future is the reinstatement of simple, colorful stuffers for pay envelopes, which have not been used for several years. Reynolds believes they are eye-catching and inexpensive, and serve as useful reminders of various aspects of the benefits programs.

The company also plans to expand and formalize its program of preretirement counseling. At present, such counseling is done informally. Those who are about to retire direct questions to any available supervisor or Personnel Department employee, or to Mr. Adams. In addition to more formal counseling before retirement, the company plans to make greater efforts to communicate with retired employees. This group currently receives *The Reynolds Review*, which gives them news of the company as well as information about changes in benefits. Letters to their homes explain changes which affect them, and occasionally their pension checks include descriptive stuffers.

Schering Corporation

Schering, a pharmaceuticals manufacturer, is headquartered in Bloomfield, New Jersey, with approximately 9 North American and 27 international locations and a personnel strength of 8,000 (4,000 in the United States). Compensation and benefits are managed on the corporate level by H. C. Lundquist, whose office operates under that of the director of employee relations.

Schering's chief purpose in communicating information about benefits is to instill in employees a thorough understanding of what they are entitled to. Mr. Lundquist feels that Schering's benefits, among them plans of profit sharing, health and life insurance, retirement, vacations, disability compensation, and free company products, serve both to attract new employees to the company and to retain and inspire loyalty in current employees. Schering believes in a communications program of complete information to all employees, "totally aboveboard" as Mr. Lundquist describes it.

The Employee Relations and Public Relations Departments, both under the direction of the vice-president of administrative services, work jointly to plan and execute this program. The company's annual report is prepared principally by the Public Relations Department, while the quarterly magazine and biweekly employee newspaper are developed by both departments. The Employee Relations Department is the prime developer and updater of the *Employee Handbook*, as well as the originator of letters to employees' homes. Computerized annual statements of profit-sharing and pension-plan statistics are prepared by a bank.

The greatest amount of effort and money for benefits communications at Schering is expended on printed materials. The *Employee Handbook*, which contains illustrated explanations of Schering's various benefit plans and the full, official texts of insurance, retirement, and profit-sharing plans, is stressed as the current all-inclusive reference source. The handbook is in the form of a looseleaf binder, to which pages containing updated information are added, and an entirely new handbook is reproduced every two years.

Articles concerning benefits appear occasionally in the biweekly employee newspaper, particularly when changes are imminent. Bulletin boards are used for quick communications, and pay envelope stuffers briefly announce changes in Social Security, taxes, and so on. The predominant medium for informing employees personally of modifications in their benefits is a letter which is sent to their homes. A great effort is made in these letters to involve employees' families in those benefits which most affect them—company product privileges, group life and health insurance, profit sharing, and pensions. Computerized statements of the last two are also sent directly to the homes.

New participants in the profit-sharing and pension plans are indoctrinated in small seminars; at least one of these is held each year at all locations in the United States. Flip charts and slides are sometimes used to supplement verbal material and printed handouts.

Quarterly management meetings are held for Schering's exempt employees, during which explanations of benefits are sometimes presented to increase the participants' familiarity with them. Throughout the year, employees at most locations meet in small groups with personnel and plant managers. A variety of subjects are discussed, and questions about benefits arise frequently. When brief oral answers cannot be given, the questions are researched at the corporate level. Answers are written on question-and-answer sheets which are returned to the employee as quickly as possible. These sheets are frequently disseminated on a broad basis for employees' general information.

In addition to finding out what employees think about their benefits through such meetings, the company employs an outside organization to administer occasional opinion surveys. Several hundred people in one Schering location were surveyed about benefits three years ago. The findings eventually led to a noncontributory pension plan and a long-term disability plan.

Individual preretirement counseling is available to all employees at the age of 62, and employees are usually eager to participate. Options from which they may choose under their pension and profit-sharing plans, details of Social Security benefits, and a bit of estate planning are among the subjects covered in these counseling sessions. After retirement (there are currently some 250 retirees), the company stays in touch through an annual retirees' dinner. Retirees are kept on the mailing list for regular publications, and they also receive yearly an updated address directory of all Schering retirees. They are still eligible for company product privileges and noncontributory major medical insurance (above and beyond Medicare).

Schering's benefits budget, which includes expenditures for benefits communications, has increased significantly in the past several years. The quarterly employee magazine, *Schering People*, is relatively new, and the employee newspaper is just five years old. Mr. Lundquist says, "There is always some degree to which benefits communications can be improved to educate employees completely." He would especially like to see further improvements of oral communications procedures, with more in-depth training of those who lead employee groups in discussions about benefits. Informality reigns at Schering, however, in the belief that a relaxed approach stimulates more open two-way communication on all subjects. There are no plans for a more formal structure of communications programs.

Appendix

Summary of Benefits Communications Practices in 202 Large Companies

IN developing material for this book, 430 major American business and industrial organizations were asked to fill out questionnaires dealing with the media, expenditures, philosophies, and personnel involved in their efforts to communicate information about benefits to their employees. Forty-seven percent of those surveyed responded. The greatest number of answers came from organizations in the electrical/electronics machinery industry (see Figure 4).

Figure 4. Industrial Classification of Survey Respondents

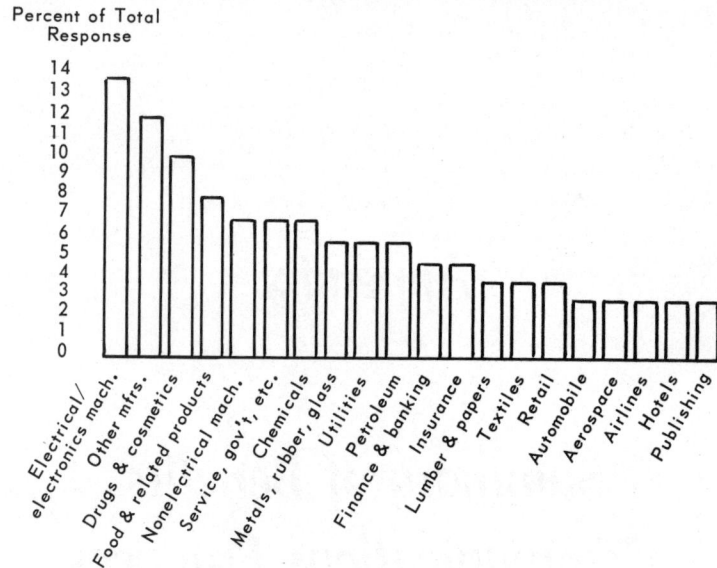

Percent of Total Response

[Bar chart showing classifications from left to right: Electrical/electronics mach., Other mfrs., Drugs & cosmetics, Food & related products, Nonelectrical mach., Service, gov't, etc., Chemicals, Metals, rubber, glass, Utilities, Petroleum, Finance & banking, Insurance, Lumber & papers, Textiles, Retail, Automobile, Aerospace, Airlines, Hotels, Publishing]

Classification

Survey questions focused on the following points:

- Objectives of the company's benefits communications program.
- Organizational functions responsible for employee benefits communications and the production of related materials.
- Primary techniques and media used by companies to communicate information about benefits to their employees.
- Primary techniques and media used by companies to gather feedback information from their employees.

- Retirement counseling programs and their presentation.
- Annual expenditures per employee for benefits communication.
- Challenges and changes in communicating information about benefits.

The findings of this survey revealed new trends and goals for benefits communications efforts. Although the personnel function, either singly or in combination with another function, proved to be most often responsible for these efforts, there was evidence of greater use of outside management consultants, public relations firms, or benefits-oriented organizations for direction in presenting benefits information to employees.

Techniques used to communicate data about benefits to employees were relatively uniform, with articles in in-house publications and personalized annual reports about benefits clearly the most popular media (see Figure 5). Respondents indicated an average of three different techniques each used for downward communications about benefits. Written material and meetings proved far more popular than kinetic media such as movies and television.

In garnering information about benefits from their employees (for example, degree of understanding, acceptance, problems), an overwhelming number of respondents stated that their chief method was "direct, personal access to benefits administrators." Occasional attitude surveys, meetings, suggestion devices, articles in house organs or letters or both, regularly scheduled attitude surveys, and assorted other means were reported to be used, in the above order of frequency. Respondents averaged two techniques each for upward communications. Surprisingly, several large companies indicated that they had no method

Figure 5. Most Frequently Used Techniques for Downward Communications

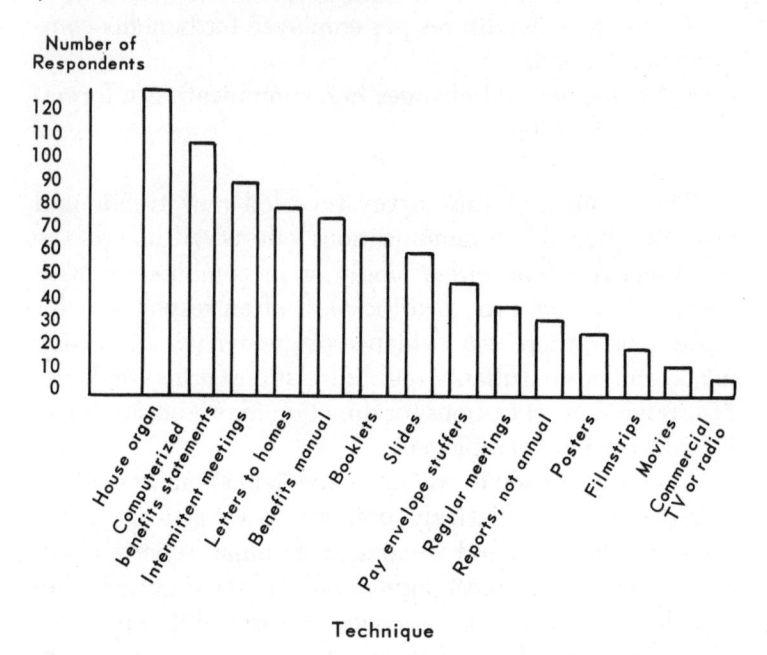

Number of Respondents / Technique

Bars (left to right): House organ; Computerized benefits statements; Intermittent meetings; Letters to homes; Benefits manual; Booklets; Slides; Pay envelope stuffers; Regular meetings; Reports, not annual; Posters; Filmstrips; Movies; Commercial TV or radio

in use for evaluating employee understanding and acceptance of company benefits and communications about them.

Preretirement counseling was not practiced by 38 percent of the respondent organizations. However, in quite a few companies, one of the more prevalent changes in benefits communications programs in the recent past has been the addition or expansion of preretirement counseling. Of those organizations who reported having such programs, a larger number began them a year or more before an employee's retirement rather than nearer the retirement date. In addition, individual counseling was more prevalent than group counseling. Published material appeared to supplement counseling in most cases. A relatively small number of organizations reported efforts at postretirement follow-up.

The majority (53%) of those responding to the questionnaire did not know the approximate annual expenditure per employee for benefits communications in their companies (see Figure 6).

Figure 6. Annual Expenditure per Employee for Benefits Communications

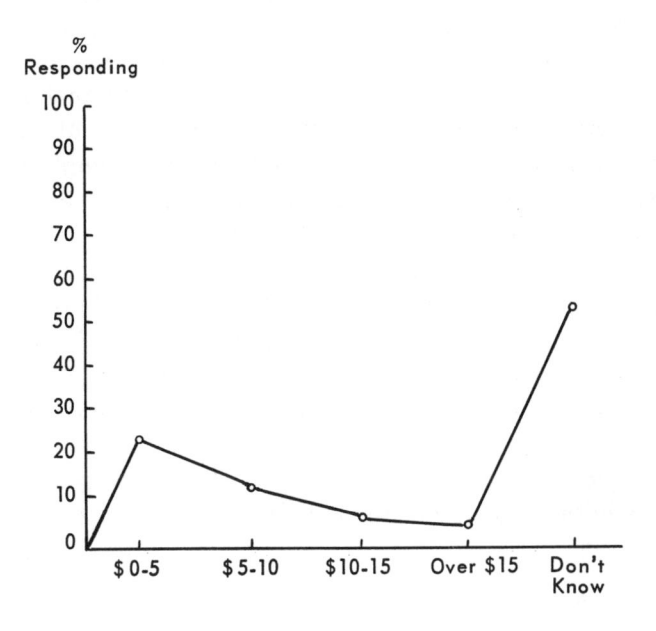

The most frequently observed change in benefits communications procedures was the personal, computerized annual statement of benefits. Most of those companies reporting recent adoption of these statements commented on their clear, concise manner of relating information about benefits to the employee in a meaningful, personal way.

To achieve this end was a primary challenge expressed by most respondents. In addition to instigating greater personal understanding of benefits by the employee himself, companies evidenced a growing desire to explain benefits more personally to employees' families. Thus, a significant increase was noted in the use of benefits-related letters sent to employees' homes, where the entire family has access to them, and a general trend toward more attention to spouses in communications about benefits and pre-retirement counseling.

The challenge of more intimate benefits communications between employer and employee is being met by plans for more frequent meetings of small groups of employees with managers. Professional gauging of employee understanding and response to benefits and the way information about them is communicated is on the increase through the use of employee surveys.

A great many companies expressed an interest in pointing out to their employees the monetary value of their benefits, with special emphasis on the companies' generosity in assuming all or part of the cost. It appears, then, that many organizations see benefits as a means of inspiring employee loyalty, and that they wish to reinforce this loyalty in their communications about benefits.